Danny and Cheryl Dean

Copyright © 2017 Danny J. Dean
All rights reserved.

Deeper Still

DEDICATION

This book is dedicated first to my father, Robert James Dean. He is my inspiration and I hope to be just like him when I grow up.

To my wife, Cheryl Anne Dean for her consistent support, love, and encouragement.

To all our children, grandchildren, and great grandchild.

To the courageous few who choose the "Road Less Traveled", the ones who cannot settle for platcaus of just enough and only a small taste of all God wants to give.

To you who are suffering and find yourself beyond your capacity to trust your own heart, feelings, and instincts.

To Yeshua my God, my Savior, and my constant companion and friend.

Deeper Still

Introduction

No doubt hundreds of books have been written addressing questions of "why". Why do the righteous suffer? Why is life often unfair? Why is there so much pain at times? Many of these books evoke sympathy and compassion. Our goal is not to focus on the "why" of suffering, but it is to show how we responded in a time of suffering and what benefit we found in total trust in God.

This is the story of our journey through the diagnosis of cancer, surgery, multiple life-threatening complications, and the road to recovery. This is also the story of how God sustained both of us and brought us through as only He could.

In this book, we share from my perspective and from Cheryl's perspective. Often our stories will overlap as we share our experience from different views.

"There is no pit so deep, that God's love is not deeper still."
Corrie ten Boom

He brought me up out of the pit of destruction, out of the miry clay, And He set my feet upon a rock making my footsteps firm.

Psalm 40:2 (NASB)

CONTENTS

Chapter 1	Don't Waste Your Sorrows – Danny
Chapter 2	Into the Fire – Danny
Chapter 3	The Dark Night of The Soul – Danny
Chapter 4	The Care Giver's Viewpoint – Cheryl
Chapter 5	The Winding Road to Recovery – Cheryl
Chapter 6	Life Flight – Cheryl
Chapter 7	Staying Tethered – Cheryl
Chapter 8	Miracle Healing – Danny
Chapter 9	The End of the Valley – Danny
Epilogue	

Deeper Still

ACKNOWLEDGMENTS

Along life's journey, there are so many experiences that help to shape our character, outlook, and world view. Of all these experiences, nothing is more powerful than the people we allow into our lives.

Cheryl A. Dean – My wife, who has helped me find the fact that we are healed through marriage and that we can choose to minister love to one another in sickness and in health.

Jesse Ball – Amazing friend and confidant through all my travels and experiences – the good, the bad and the ugly.

The Monday morning Heavenly Court Room team: Timothy and Rachel Bertsch, Sharon Ziegler, Stephanie Reiland, Paul Nesbitt, Alexis Alexander, Travis and Jenna Vaad, Dennis Crane, and Naomi Dean. Your steadfast love, prophetic words and prayers have sustained us.

Wednesday morning prayer team with Dr. Dennis Crane.

Thursday night home meeting family who stood with us with words and actions. (I will never forget the night everyone wore pajama bottoms so I wouldn't feel alone)

My Tacoma Intertribal Gathering family.

The two pillars in my life to whom I owe more than I could ever repay in a lifetime:

Dr. Bruce Cook, Chairman, Kingdom Congressional International Alliance (K.C.I.A.)

John Anderson, Chairman, Global Development Partners Ltd. (GDP)

The Kingdom Congressional International Alliance (K.C.I.A.) family.

Dad's House family, whose love and support overwhelmed our hearts. We could not have survived in so many ways without our pastor, Shawn Niles.

Lauri Russell who gave countless hours to editing this manuscript.

And Grant Russell my dear friend and encourager.

Countless hundreds of saints around the world and this nation who have remained faithful in your love, care and prayer.

Forward
By Dr. Bruce Cook

My friend Danny Dean is a warrior, among other things. He is also an apostle, prophet, intercessor, father, husband, son, and brother. When he told me last spring that he had received a diagnosis of cancer, I knew in my spirit that it was not his time to die, that he had unfulfilled prophecies and destiny for his life, and that this was not an illness or disease unto death, although the enemy of our souls tried to speak otherwise to Danny. So, I, along with many other faithful friends and family, went to war for him, on his behalf, both on earth and in the courts of heaven, in prayer and intercession, in multiple hospital visits, speaking words of life, anointing with oil and laying on of hands. (James 5:14-15)

Our attitude and posture in prayer was, no wounded warrior left behind, and no premature death or aborted destiny allowed on our watch. That may sound presumptive to some, or even arrogant, but nothing could be further from the truth. In humility, but boldness, we pleaded Danny's case in the courts of heaven, and reminded God the Father of his unfulfilled prophecies and destiny, and decreed with authority and power the word of God over his life and situation. We surrounded him with love and prayer, and covered him like a blanket. We were both vigilant and militant in our faith and prayers, as we pleaded and declared his righteous cause. God, in His infinite wisdom, mercy and grace, chose to spare his life, and grant him more years on earth, as he did King Hezekiah (Isaiah 38:5; 2 Kings 20:5-6).

These are sobering situations, and we all know those who have experienced a different outcome. The story of Danny's life and death struggle, setbacks, surrender, serenity, survival, and supernatural comeback and return to health, recovery, restoration, reformation, and renovation, is a story of courage, a story of being an overcomer, and of standing in faith when the odds look impossible, the pain is unbearable, the long dark night of the soul makes God look invisible, and the necessity of God's miraculous intervention is undeniable.

As you read Danny's story, you will doubtless see your own self in some part or all of his story, and find comfort, courage, encouragement, strength, hope and faith for your own struggle or journey. And, just remember, *"...there is a friend who sticks closer than a brother."* (Prov. 18:24, NIV) His name is Jesus, and I pray that you either know Him as both Lord and Savior of your life, or that you come to know Him in the near future through the power of the Holy Spirit.

Chapter 1

"Don't Waste Your Sorrows"

On December 16, 1980, my littlest angel, my daughter, Aubrey Lynn Grace Dean, went home to be with Jesus. Aubrey was five and half years old. On the day of the funeral, I was standing in my suit, looking out the living room window, transfixed by the beautiful sunshine on this December day, and wondered why the whole world was not standing still. As I stared out the window, I felt the gentle touch of God's hand on my shoulder and heard in my innermost being these gentle words, "There are two ways to go through what you are going through. One way is the way of grief known by the world and natural pain, or allow Me to take you through this with the constant awareness that I am at your side." At that moment, I said, "O Lord, I want to go through this with you at my side." In that instant, I felt Him place His hand on my chest. What was planted deep into my heart was the absolute and resolute conviction that I would see Aubrey again. Of all the things that I know are true, this stands out as one of the most powerful facts I hold as true and absolute. He went on to tell me there would be the pain of grief; however, together we would take each step and each day, one at a time.

At the funeral, many people spoke wonderful and comforting words. It was so good to hear people say her name, "Aubrey." Each time I heard her name mentioned, my heart would leap as if to say, "That is right; she is alive. She will not come back to me; however, I will go to her."

A man walked up to me and placed in my hands a book, *Don't Waste Your Sorrows*, by Paul E. Billheimer. Some might say, "How insensitive at such a time like this." However, it was perfect and the key I needed to unlock the joy only God can give when we live life and look at every circumstance from His eyes and His heart.

Now, 36 years later, holding this worn and faded book in my hands, just as I held it that sad day so many years ago, I am still living by what I learned. There are at least two ways to approach every situation: the natural, human way apart from God, or the supernatural, Holy Spirit way and in union with God. I chose the latter and this has become a lifestyle. I would rather go through the hard times that are a part of life with God and His amazing Grace for every situation than abandon God and tough it out on my own, relying only on my own strength and abilities.

The power of hope that was birthed in my heart on the day we laid my little angel to rest still propels me forward and enables me to live each day with anticipation and joy.

What we can do with God's love and help far surpasses all earthly and natural abilities.

There have been many hard times since Aubrey's passing, including the sense that I believed I would die of a broken heart when my first marriage ended after 18 years.

In life, there have always been challenges. Good times and bad times. Good decisions and the consequences of bad choices. I have had more than my fair share of all these. There have been times when I sat down and wept over failures. There have been times when I ran with all my might after this dream or that. There have been times when I walked away from God thinking I could do a better job on my own.

Through it all, since the day I asked Jesus to come into my heart and be the Lord of my life, He has always been there. After sincere repentance and the sorrow of failing to live up to His love and righteousness, He has always embraced me as if I were an only son. His words to me have always been, "I forgive you, I love you and now let's get on with the destiny - this destiny that I have always had planned for you."

I have applied my heart to study God's Word and learn who He is, who I truly am, and what my destiny is. I chose to surrender all that I am or ever hope to be to Him. I leave my life in His hands and now choose to free fall in total faith in Him.

Life happens and it is not personal, it is just life. I have learned "Extreme Ownership" in regard to my responsibility for my life. This means there has never been anyone else to blame for my mistakes and I choose always and in every situation to find

Jesus in it. He is there always; we just have to look for Him.

As a teacher of the Word of God and a minister of His love and Grace, every lesson I taught or learned became very real when the doctor said in March 2016, "It is cancer!"

Chapter 2

Into the Fire – Danny

"When you pass through the waters, I will be with you." (Isaiah 43:2, NASB)

It was a beautiful early spring day in 2016. So much excitement in the air. Soon, our dear friends, Lana and Kevin Vawser, from Brisbane, Australia, would be in our home for a week. Plans were all coming together for a luncheon, home church meetings, and a big Aglow gathering on Saturday. It was one of those times when everything seemed to be falling into place and the blessings of the Lord just seemed to keep mounting.

One of the greatest joys in my life was to look out over a well-manicured lawn, a house all ready for many out of town guests, and the general sense of anticipation.

Being right in at the center of all this activity filled my heart to overflowing. I was teaching a Saturday morning class on basic doctrine and led a home group in our house. Everything in life was beautiful and full of joy.

The only thing that was not quite right was that my appetite began to decrease.

Nearly two weeks before all the big events, I woke up early and began to prepare for the day. Looking into the mirror, I was sure something was wrong with the lighting. My skin had a yellow cast to it.

At this time, I weighed 213 pounds with a 38-inch waist. This would change dramatically over the next five months.

Over the next two days, my wife, Cheryl, noticed it too. Something was not right; I was jaundiced. After visiting our local doctor for blood tests, we received a call from his office, "Proceed immediately to the emergency room." So, began an intense six-month ordeal.

We went to our local hospital in Yakima, Washington. After medical consultation, the decision was made--we needed to be sent to a hospital in Seattle for a procedure. The local hospital did not have the resources available for my condition, and it was determined that I would need to be transported two and a half hours to a very large hospital, Virginia Mason, in Seattle. This hospital had the skilled staff and facilities to treat the most difficult illnesses. It was determined that I would be transported via ambulance according to protocol for such situations. Cheryl followed in her car.

We knew that something was blocking a bile duct leading from my liver. Our hope at that time was that the blockage would be removed and then I would go on with life.

The procedure to put a temporary stent in the duct went smoothly and successfully. Cheryl and I returned to Yakima and, satisfied the crisis was over, we continued to prepare for the week's events with Lana and Kevin. The excitement was tremendous as we were all ready for the arrival of our guests - including our dear friends from Perth, Australia; Gig Harbor, Washington; and the local community.

The week was wonderful and included a luncheon home meeting led by Lana, and then a spectacular citywide Aglow meeting. We went to the local Christian TV station to tape an interview with Dr. Bruce Cook and Lana Vawser. It was my privilege to host and conduct the interview, which focused on what it means to be a prophet and why this ministry is important today. So many friends were around us and we enjoyed this wonderful time.

The gathering was amazing and yet behind the scenes was the concern for the results of my procedure. During one session, as the house was filled with people listening to Lana, one of our friends Angela Sprester, abruptly left the meeting. At the time, it was curious but we quickly forgot about it. (See Epilogue)

A few days later, the phone rang. The doctor who had accomplished the procedure to unblock the bile duct, called to inform us what was causing the blockage. It was cancer. Surgery would be required to remove it.

Amazingly, I was not surprised. I shared the results with Cheryl and we began to look immediately to the Lord for His word on the matter. I heard Him say, "You will go through the surgery; however, you will come through it. You will be okay." Cheryl, independent of myself, also heard the exact same word in her spirit. This word would become an anchor for us both over the months that followed and the challenges yet to unfold before us.
At this time, a funny thought went through my mind, "It isn't an angry tumor."

We shared the diagnosis with a few of our guests and immediately everyone went to prayer for us. With all the meetings over, our guests began to return to their homes. For Cheryl and me, we were left with the quiet home again and our thoughts. We knew that Jesus was in this situation, all we had to do was find Him. We began to ask, "What does this mean and what should we do?" The peace of God settled over us and together we faced the difficult journey that lay before us. We clung to the assurance that God was well aware of our situation and He had made it clear I would come through this. One of the greatest gifts that God gives us is His peace and calm assurance; He would be with us every step along the way.

We drove to Seattle and began to prepare our hearts and minds for the surgery that would take place the next day, on March 29th. We checked into a hotel next to the hospital, The Baroness. It seemed like a mini-vacation at this point.

The surgery was scheduled to last four to five hours. The staff prepared me for the surgery and I had a moment of a panic as the time to begin the sedatives quickly approached. There are some responses to a crisis that are natural and very understandable; yet for us, we kept our hearts focused on what God promised, "You will come through this and you will be okay."

I woke up in intensive care and felt very comfortable. An epidural pain blocker had been inserted in my spine and therefore, I had no pain whatsoever. I continued to feel comfortable as the nurses and patient care technicians kept a constant watch on my recovery from surgery in the ICU. What normally should have been a straight forward four to five-hour surgery took nine hours, became a surgery with extensive complications encountered during the procedure.

This was not pancreatic cancer, but the tumor was near the pancreas and required a surgery on par with a liver transplant in complexity for resolution. We were informed that with any surgery of this type, there is always the possibility of complications.

Over the next three days, the health care was excellent and recovery had begun. On the fourth day after surgery, I was moved to the next level of care and a new room. I was informed that the team which had placed the epidural would be coming by to remove it. There was no problem on my part as I felt no pain whatsoever.

However, when the epidural was removed, there was no warm transfer for pain management and I was unaware of any potential for pain. Steve and Tina McCorkle, from Bonney Lake First Fruits Ministry, came to visit shortly after the epidural was removed. As our visit began, suddenly a pain greater than anything I could possibly imagine shot through my body. I lost all sense of my surroundings as my body shuddered under the excruciating pain that took over all my senses.

At that moment, I threw up my arms and shouted, at the top of my lungs, "JESUS, YOU REMAIN WORTHY OF ALL MY PRAISE AND ALL MY WORSHIP!" At this point, a nurse walked in and immediately knew something was terribly wrong. She returned with a shot of something, and suddenly, I didn't feel any more pain. Of course, my eyes rolled back in my head and I became loopy; but at least I didn't feel pain any more.

The McCorkles said that in all their experiences in church and all the glorious worship services they had attended in the past, nothing compared to the Glory that filled that room when my shout of worship went up to the Lord.

A week after the surgery, my recovery was going well and it was determined we could go home. What joy as we started the two-and-a-half-hour drive back to Yakima. The worst was behind us, or so we thought.

Over the next few days, my appetite continued to be non-existent. The days were filled with rest and recuperation. Pain control medication was needed and my strength was gone. Often, I would stare across the room at a book or the TV controller with no strength to move to pick them up. Cheryl and my daughter Naomi became my constant care givers, whether it was a need for water or help walking to the bathroom. I had to sit in the shower on a stool as there was no strength to stand up. The weakness and chills left me even less capable of taking care of myself.

A week and a half later, we returned to the hospital for a checkup where a test showed that I was running a high fever. The doctor decided at that moment to admit me back into the hospital. We were not prepared for this. Once again, the hospital routine began with the regular shots in the belly to prevent blood clots in the legs and regular trips to the CT Scan technicians to check on internal conditions.

Doctors determined there was an infection and so a regimen of anti-biotics began. At one point the medicine pole next to me looked like a Christmas tree with so many bags. The treatment began for the infection and also for severe heartburn. The profound weakness and pain was beyond my capacity to cope or control. Literally my life and existence was in the hands of God, the medical staff and my dear wife who slept in the room by my side.

It was determined that I needed to have a drainage tube installed in my side with a drainage bag to collect the infectious matter.

Oftentimes I would whisper to the Lord my desire to lay my head upon His chest and confess my joy that He was my hope and my life line. Life more than ever became one breath at a time, one heartbeat, and one minute at a time. There were no thoughts about the future or what I was to do next. The only thoughts I had were in this now moment and how He had to carry me from one procedure and each treatment process to the next.
As each heartbeat led to another and each event moved along, never once did I feel like a victim. How could I, since it is no longer I who lives but Christ in me. Never once did I ask, "Why me?" The question was not, "Why me?" It could only be, "Why not me?" Never once did I fall into self-pity. Every word we have taught and every lesson we have declared became a reality. If God is real in the good times when everything is easy and we can't find Him in the hard times, then we are to be pitied. If He is real to us in the worship service when everything is going our way and we then throw away our confidence and the intimacy we have learned to love in the hard times, then our faith is based on something other than the reality of who God is and our relationship with Him.

Everything is easy when it is easy. Worship and praise are wonderful and one of our greatest joys. However, when the crisis comes and life circumstances are filled with pain, reversal and physical agony, where do we turn? When the realities of our faith are on the line, this is when we prove His Word is true and He is who He says He is.

Choosing to turn into God, believe in Him and having faith in the middle of the fire, when you have no control over your own body or the events unfolding around you, is where God and your relationship with Him become the only reality to hold on to.

There was no feeling of God's presence; however, when I turned my heart to God, I found the comfort of His peace deep in my heart. This peace was there before the illness set in. Because I deeply knew the Lord prior to these events, I knew He would be there and every word of the Book of Heaven (The Bible) was true now more than ever. He wrote my story before I was born according to Psalm 139. This story was a poem He wrote, and this was just one chapter in the book.

This Scripture at the beginning of these events became my rallying cry and declaration:

"Now I rejoice in my sufferings for your sake, and in my flesh, I do my share on behalf of His body, which is the church, in filling up what is lacking in Christ's afflictions." (Colossians 1:24, NASB)

The issue was never me; it was what is God doing and what does all this mean? If we are going to preach and teach concepts, then we must know they are true not only in the good times but also when everything is going wrong and your strength is gone, when pain rises and you are losing weight at an accelerated rate.

I found that I could not eat at all. Nothing tasted good and there was no appetite. Over this time and during the next events that were about to unfold, I lost 63 pounds and could not eat. My body reacted with severe nausea and gagging if I attempted to put food or any fluids in my mouth.

We became very grateful for the many doctors, nurses and patient care technologists that provided compassionate care. One of our PCTs was from Nigeria and his name was "ThankGod." It was awesome to see him and yell, "ThankGod, how are you doing?"

Our dear Native American friend from the Quinault Tribe, Melvin Hoage, and his wife, Becky, showered us with love and regular visits to the hospital. The blanket they gave me was my constant comfort and provided warmth. The hand-carved wooden necklace was a reminder of the journey ahead. We didn't know what was yet to come.

Chapter 3

The Dark Night of the Soul – Danny

Of all the sounds of weeping and the groans of loss and suffering, few know that before there was one human being, it was God who was weeping. And it was His tears that filled the seas for He knew we would suffer in this life and the sorrows we would bear. He chose to walk among us as a man so that He himself could say, "I know how you feel; I have felt it too." God goes beyond sympathy and compassion into the depths of empathy.

Once again, it was determined that I was well enough to go home. Once again, we took that long drive back to Yakima.

At home, I had no strength to go up the steps to our bedroom and had to sleep downstairs in a spare bedroom. Finally, with Cheryl's help, I worked my way up the steps.

We were not home long before something changed and I slipped into another crisis. Quickly we called 911 and my bedroom was filled with EMTs. There was profound distress as my body screamed in agony.

The EMTs took a dining room chair and moved me to it. They carried me down the stairs and to the ambulance. Once again, I was transported to the local hospital and once again it was determined I needed to be taken to the hospital in Seattle immediately. I was transported via ambulance to Seattle. After spending a week in the hospital, with successful efforts to stabilize me, it was determined I had recovered from the most recent crisis so we returned to Yakima.

Within a day of being home, I began to bleed when I went to the bathroom. Within a few days, my situation worsened as I also began to throw up blood.

We called 911 and I was once again carried to the ambulance on the dining room chair. This time, the ambulance driver turned on his lights and siren as I was rushed to Memorial Hospital. This time it was critical. I was given a pint of blood and arrangements were made for the Life Flight Helicopter to fly me to Seattle. Lying there in the emergency room with the lights turned down very low, I had a tent of sorts was over my head and was surrounded by praying saints. I was critical and everyone knew it.

During the flight, I became very aware of the spirit of death as it entered the helicopter. I said, "You don't intimidate me." And promptly I heard that still small voice of the Lord say, "You are going to be fine; you are not done yet." The helicopter ride took forty-five minutes before we landed in the cold night air atop Virginia Mason Hospital. Once I was back in the hospital, additional blood and plasma were administered to stabilize me.

It was determined there was bleeding from some veins near the surgery area. This needed to be repaired by an angioplasty procedure to prevent these veins from bleeding. The secretions of the pancreas had eaten away a few veins to release the blood. Once again, I was wheeled into a very cold operating room and anesthetized. Gratefully, this procedure was a success and the recovery process began.

Once I was back at home, I still could not eat and the weight continued to drop pound after pound.

Every attempt to turn this around failed. We were told that it was not uncommon for this to happen and there was no explanation as to why it happens or why people begin to eat again.

We began attempting to introduce protein drinks. Nothing was really helping and protein drinks tasted disgusting to me. I dreaded the thought of these attempts to get me to eat. My concerned wife told me to hold my nose and just force it down. Nothing worked and I found myself not wanting to even try.

Our friend, Stephanie Reiland, would come over a few times a week and massage my feet and pray over me. What a comfort and something to look forward to. Between the massage and gentle music playing, it provided an hour to relax and enjoy the presence of the Lord as visions and experiences in the Spirt lifted my heart. What a comfort and generous gift this was when I was physically and emotionally drained.

One afternoon I crawled up on the massage table and said, "Here I am Lord; I present my body as a living sacrifice here before You." My prayer was, "All that I am or ever hope to be is now and always will be in You. I am not my own. I am Yours completely."

I wept as I said, "Lord I only have enough strength to lay my head on Your shoulder."

I was under the constant care and attentive love of my wife. Cheryl had to do nurse duty and was a constant encourager, reminding me what the Lord had said, "You will get through this, you will be ok." Naomi was on nurse duty when Cheryl was at her teaching job.

My local church took on the prayer burden in significant ways. Soon after the diagnosis was established and the surgery scheduled, they began to pray and show us their deep love and concern. They stood beside us as we entered the darkest hours.

Support and prayers and words of encouragement began to flow in from around the world. Friends in South Africa, Great Britain, Perth and Brisbane, Australia, and Canada reached out. My dear brother in the Lord in Minnesota, Jesse Ball, would send audio texts with words of encouragement. Friends would stop by the house many times during the week. Some would call on a regular basis to see how I was doing and to pray for me. Text messages, emails, and Facebook posts poured in during the dark days and months. We were overwhelmed by the love and support we received.

Many gifts were brought to us. Our pastor, Shawn Niles (who later appeared on Master Chef) cooked a meal for the family; unfortunately, I was the only one who was unable to enjoy his efforts.

There is nothing like being loved and cared for. When we invest our lives in others, it produces the fruit that comes back when we need it the most. Not that this is the motivation; however, by being other-centered with true love, it is like sowing into a beautiful garden that is there to enjoy when you need it the most.

Cheryl missed many days of work and lost income. An account was set up online and people began to give generously. As a result, all our needs were met. We will never be able to say thank you enough for the amazing generosity.

Chapter 4

The Caregiver's Viewpoint – Cheryl

"I would have despaired unless I had believed that I would see the goodness of the Lord in the land of the living." (Psalm 27:13, NASB)

This is a lot harder to write than I thought it would be. As Danny's wife and chief caregiver through the storm of the past six months of surgery and recovery, the Lord gave me courage and stamina beyond belief. Now that the storm has calmed, although not yet finished, I am experiencing what many have assured me is very common when a person has gone through a very traumatic experience—Post Traumatic Stress Disorder (PTSD). Through God's strength and the prayers of family and friends, I was buoyed with the strength and calmness to do what I had to do at the time. Now that the hardest parts were over, the shock, pain, stress, loss, and heartache began to come upon me. I was sad and didn't know why. Shouldn't I be happy? My husband is still alive and the school year (stressful) is over. Why do I feel depressed?

It was a relief when I found out these feelings were common and that I would get over them. I started to heal emotionally over a few weeks and through the support of friends, I discovered it was okay to grieve after the fact, even though our outcome from this trauma had been favorable. Just when I was feeling somewhat back to normal emotionally, I sat down to write this book with Danny. To get a timeline for the journey, I began to read my journal, along with texts between my sister, Judy Johnston, and myself. I cried tears of joy at my sister's great encouragement to me and tears of grief as I allowed myself to feel the trauma once again.

I believe that remembering the trauma will help me heal and remind me of the goodness of God, but the main reasons I write this is for those who are going through trauma or loss or sickness, and for those who are healing from these things. I pray that any caregivers will be encouraged by what I've been through and how I got through it. And I pray that any patients will understand the caregiver's viewpoint. I also pray that anyone who is watching a family go through traumatic sickness will have empathy and an understanding of ways they can help. Hold on to the word of God and any rhema word he has given you; accept the prayers and support of your family and friends; rest when you need it; and remember that God loves you and He is in all this.

Danny and I had only been married for three years when the commitment we made to stick together "in sickness and health" was tested. We were no strangers to trials and loss before we married: I had lost a brother, sister, and a niece who all died at early ages. I was also dealing with a 26-year illness, Rheumatoid Arthritis, and had gone through the divorce of my parents as well as my own divorce (which was like a death). Danny, as he shared, had the unfathomable loss of a five-year old daughter and had also gone through divorce. We understood heartache, but Danny's illness was the first trial we experienced together.

In February of 2016, in the middle of organizing a weeklong visit of a speaker and her family from Australia, Danny began to feel nausea and his appetite dwindled. This went on for several weeks when he began to experience abdominal pain. Ever the concerned wife, I recommended he see the doctor pronto. As he waited for his doctor appointment, his pain became more severe and I commented that his eyes looked a little yellow. Still, my cool, calm, collected husband waited for his doctor appointment. I came home from my teaching job one evening (yes, I am a crazy middle school language arts teacher!) and Danny stepped into the room saying, "Do I look yellow?" I stared in disbelief at my now yellow husband! "I think you need to go see the doctor right away!" I said in my concerned wife voice. He insisted he could wait for his appointment the next day.

The general practitioner ran some tests and sent Danny home as he waited results. The following day, March 3rd, 2016, I had just started my school day when our pastor, Shawn, called on my classroom phone to tell me Danny had gone to the emergency room at a hospital in Yakima and that Danny didn't want me to worry and I probably didn't need to come to the hospital. Of course, I worried and immediately began contacting my school's office to ask for a sub. I was shaking as I told my students what was happening and tried to make sub plans. My mind just wouldn't stay focused as thoughts raced through my head. "What was so urgent that he had to go to emergency? What does he have? How fast do I need to get there?"

I drove up to Memorial's emergency room. Pastor Shawn was already there with his toddler son. Danny was sitting in his hospital bed, yellow, but jovial and energetic. He said that the doctor's office had read the results of his tests and told him to get to emergency right away. Danny's friend, Paul Stadler, showed up for support, as well as Shawn's wife, Tenielle, who had come to pick up their son. We prayed with Danny, then chatted and even joked with the nurses. The atmosphere of the room was strangely festive because we had no idea of the trial to come and we had the assurance that God was in the situation. When Danny was rolled away in the gurney to have a CT scan, the gravity of the situation hit me. With tears in my eyes, I told the pastor and his wife that it took me a long time to find this amazing man and now that I found him, I couldn't bear losing him. They held my hands and prayed a blanket of peace would cover me through this. I truly believe this blanket of peace stayed on me through the next six months and covered me when I needed it.

Shortly after Danny was wheeled back into the emergency room, the doctor came in with the CT results. The doctor was relieved that it didn't look like Danny had pancreatic cancer, but something was blocking the bile duct connected to the pancreas. This explained why Danny's bilirubin was high and why he looked like big bird (Danny is

6' 2" by the way.) The doctor believed it was probably some kind of stone. Since Memorial had no one who could do the procedure to remove the stone, Danny was going to be sent to Virginia Mason Hospital in Seattle, which had one of the best gastroenterology departments in the nation. Because Danny had already been admitted to the emergency room in Yakima, he had to be taken by ambulance to Virginia Mason—some rule about not being admitted to two different emergency rooms. I ran home to pack for a few days at the hospital and called in for a substitute teacher. I made the 2-and-a-half-hour drive to Seattle in record time and met Danny in his hospital room.

Danny received a more thorough CT scan and was scheduled for an ERCP the next day. The Endoscopic retrograde cholangiopancreatography - one of many long-worded procedures we were about to encounter. In laymen's terms: the surgeon put a tube with a camera and microscopic knife down Danny's throat to the bile duct going into his pancreas in hopes of removing the blockage. Before this whole ordeal began and Danny just barely knew something was wrong, the Lord had told him that he was going to the hospital, but he would get through this.

In the morning, after a night of tossing and turning, we were moved to a room on the 15th floor with an amazing view of Seattle and Lake Union. I snapped a picture of the gorgeous view and posted an update of Danny on Facebook. This was the first of many photos I would post on Facebook which I thought was way better than posting a picture of my sick, yellow husband. People came to expect that if Cheryl posted a picture of the Seattle skyline, she was giving an update on Danny. While Danny was in the procedure, my sister texted me, "Jesus is with you." When Danny was coming out of the anesthesia, I told him his wife was here—Gina Lollobrigida (a beautiful actress from the 60s). Later, while he was still groggy, I asked him if he knew who his wife is. "Yah," he grinned, "Gina Lollobrigida!"

At this point, the doctor came in and told us that it wasn't a stone in the bile duct after all. He had put a stent in to open the duct and the bilirubin should level off with the open flow. Then the doctor said that something was cinching off the bile duct. There was a possibility of the culprit being cancer. What? Did he just say the C word? Did he just say that Danny could have cancer—the same thing that took my brother's life at the young age of 30?

That evening, Dr. Alseidi, the head surgeon in the gastroenterology department at Virginia Mason, stopped in to talk to us. He had gone to Afghanistan through the Doctors Without Borders organization which gave us confidence in his abilities and in his kindness. He gently but straightforwardly informed us of the strong possibility of the blockage being caused by cancer. In fact, he couldn't imagine that it wouldn't be. He said that since Danny was healthy overall and that he was young (66 is young?), with surgery, the prognosis looked good. Danny and I were surprisingly calm as we chose to free-fall into whatever God had planned for us.

While back at home, we went on with life with a little less yellow in it. I went back to stressful job of teaching the rowdy munchkins reading and language arts and Danny went back to retirement and the myriad of activities he was a part of—including our weekly home group and planning the events for the visit of Lana Vawser and her family. Lana is a speaker/ prophet who has been a friend of Danny's for years and was touring the US. Danny had already arranged her visit to Yakima and wanted to follow through even though he was feeling horrible. As we waited for the results of the tests, Danny was his usual calm self as he stayed in the secret place with Jesus. Since I was not good at staying in the secret place, I was concerned and thought on and off again about the pending test results. Amazingly, I wasn't the worry-wart I usually am—just concerned. I believe that the "blanket of peace" that our pastor and his wife had prayed for me was still covering me with blessed assurance. In the midst of all of this, I heard the Holy Spirit say, "It is cancer..." (I sucked in my breath) "...but he will get through this," the still, small voice continued.

That evening, the doctor called with the test results—cancer. I was surprisingly calm and told Danny that I had already been told by the Holy Spirit, that it was cancer, but that I also had been assured that he would get through it. At this point, we prayed together and continued to free fall in God's will for our lives.

According to the website "Cancer Treatment Centers of America", here is a definition of the rare type of cancer Danny was dealing with: "A rare gastrointestinal cancer, Ampullary Cancer develops in the ampulla of Vater, where the bile and pancreatic ducts meet and empty into the small intestine." If the cancer had been in Danny's pancreas (which the ampulla of Vater feeds into), symptoms of the tumor most likely would have gone unnoticed (as in most pancreatic cancer) and would have more likely ended in death within five years. Because the tumor was in the bile duct, Danny had the obvious symptoms of nausea, abdominal pain, and yellowing of his skin (high bilirubin). We were so grateful that we had caught the cancer early.

Danny's surgery was scheduled for March 29th –the week after our guests from Australia were due to leave and the week before my Spring break from school. I was feeling overwhelmed by all the preparations for surgery, substitute teacher plans, and the out of town visitors, when I had this text conversation with my biggest encourager, my sister, Judy:

iMessage Message received from Cheryl Dean 3/14/2016 4:05:14 PM
I've got to do a lot of sub planning. Would you please pray for me right now? I'm so overwhelmed, I can't even think straight. I have

so many things to do I can't even think of what to do next. I feel like my brain is shut down and my heart is racing.

iMessage Message sent by Judy 3/14/2016 4:08:33 PM
Can you step away from your desk for a moment? Or close your eyes? Do you have privacy? Close your eyes and sing "Great is Thy Faithfulness" while I pray for you!

iMessage Message received from Cheryl Dean 3/14/2016 4:10:28 PM
In my classroom alone. Was trying to deep breath. Ok. Will try to sing

iMessage Message sent Judy 3/14/2016 4:14:19 PM
God is sending you a blanket of peace; Jesus robe of righteousness is draping your shoulders and He is lifting your head! You are His child, deeply loved and cherished. When you are done singing clear off your desk even if things have to go in the floor and just put one thing at a time in front of you to do. God will carry you. And enable you. He hasn't given you a spirit of fear or panic; He is lifting you on wings of eagles so that you may run and not grow weary!

iMessage Message sent by Judy 3/14/2016 4:15:42 PM
I wish I lived nearby; I would come help you with your lesson plans. God is your help and His is able to deal with everything concerning you!!!

I was so grateful for my sister.

I had kept my 7th and 8th grade students up to date on what was happening with Danny. Most students were concerned and would ask how he was doing. One morning, a student who had been out for a while asked "Did your husband die yet?" I don't believe this student was really trying to be heartless, just an unthinking middle schooler. But I was shocked to the core---shocked that he even asked the question, and shocked that the reality was that my husband could die from this. I was physically shaking after this encounter, but pushed through the rest of the day.

Kevin and Lana Vawser and their two adorable sons visited Yakima in mid-March. We had meetings and luncheons and huge crowds over to our home. In the middle of it all, we took time out for fun by playing Xbox sports games and by taking the Vawsers to Yakima Dozer Days where the boys got to drive real bulldozers (with the assistance of an adult). The family was charming and fun—a welcome distraction from the impending surgery. When Lana spoke at the Aglow meeting, the part that stayed with me was the importance of intimacy with Jesus. If we seek to stay intimate with Jesus, we will hear his voice more and feel his presence. I knew I needed the presence of my Savior now more than ever. I needed to stay intimate with Him.
Our doctor friend, Sunny Bhaskaran, visited our home to pray for us before the surgery. We talked a long while about healing, God's desire for us to be healed, and why some people experience

miraculous healing and others do not. Dr. Sunny has travelled extensively in ministry and has been a part of many healings. He gave his testimony about his daughter's miraculous birth even though others thought she wouldn't survive. He said that after his life experiences with healings and after much research through the Bible, he believes that because Jesus was whipped for our healing, we need to accept that healing just as we accepted our salvation. Isaiah 53:5 (KJV) states, "...with his stripes, we are healed." I already knew that verse well and believed Danny and I could be healed, but the idea that we should consciously accept this free gift just like we did when we accepted our salvation was a new concept. So, in our living room, we prayed with Dr. Sunny. Danny accepted the gift of healing for Ampullary Cancer and I accepted the gift of healing for Rheumatoid Arthritis. We even envisioned ourselves taking that gift from Jesus as He freely offered it.

The day before we left for surgery, Danny and I walked up to the plateau by our home. The plateau was filled with sagebrush and tiny spring flowers and gave us a panoramic view of the Yakima Valley, Union Gap, Mt. Adams, and the snowy top of Mt. Rainier. We held hands as we walked and softly talked about life and what was up ahead. As we embraced, the wind blew tenderly through our hair. The Holy Spirit was with us. We knew that God loved us and was for us...no matter the outcome.

On March 28th, we drove from Yakima, over Snoqualmie Pass, over Lake Washington, and into downtown Seattle. We checked our baggage into the Baroness Hotel across the street from the Virginia Mason Hospital surgery center. I began taking pictures of the 1931 hotel and the area on my phone camera. I admired the hotel's structure and marveled at the first spring tulips. This was the beginning of my photo journal which would span the next few months' events. It turns out this was good therapy for me and took my mind off how stressful things really were. Taking pictures of my surroundings helped me look from the outside in and helped me look for the beauty of God's world when illness and multiple hospitalizations could have really taken a toll on me.

That evening, we met our friends from Perth, Australia, Grant and Lauri Russell, for dinner at the Virginia Mason Inn Café. Danny's appetite was still very meager but the company was great as we spent time with our "mates". This was just the beginning of the friends and family who would visit us, take us in, bring us food, send us messages of hope, respond to our Facebook posts, and send up prayers for Danny and me over the next few months.

The next day, we checked in to the surgery center. After Danny was prepped with his hospital gown and lovely surgical hair net, he got a little panicky and was given something to relax him. I felt like something calming would be a good idea for me too but still felt surprisingly calm. For anyone who knows me, calmness is not really my strong point. It was bred in me to worry and start letting the "What ifs?" swirl in my mind. I was still wearing that blanket of peace. I was sent to the waiting room to wait for what was supposed to be a 4 to 5-hour surgery where I was given a number and a beeper. I could watch a reader board to find out what was happening to my patient (surgery prep, in surgery, recovery etc.).

This is probably a good place to give you some technical information on the surgery Danny underwent--the Whipple Procedure. It sounds simple enough and maybe even a tender thing since it sounded like Mr. Whipple—the gentle store clerk who wouldn't let people "squeeze the Charmin" toilet paper in the old TV commercial. Not exactly. According to WebMD, here's the definition of a Whipple Procedure: "Also known as pancreaticoduodenectomy, the Whipple procedure involves removal of the "head" (wide part) of the pancreas next to the first part of the small intestine (duodenum). It also involves removal of the duodenum, a portion of the common bile duct, and gallbladder." Fortunately, Danny already had his gallbladder removed in a near death experience years ago. Every time I looked at that scar, I was reminded of how blessed I was to have Danny in my life. The doctor planned on following his gallbladder scar plus cutting a bit more. It was amazing to me that so much had to be taken out of him even though the cancer was miniscule at this point. The wait began....

My sister helped keep my mind at ease with the following texts:

iMessage Message sent by Judy 3/29/2016 7:37:47 AM
God goes before you and is your rearguard! He is mighty to save and delights over you with singing!

iMessage Message received from Cheryl Dean 3/29/2016 8:27:00 AM
He just had a bit of an anxiety attack. We have been calm about all this until that point. I just left him in surgery prep. They're giving him an epidural and taking him in to surgery.

iMessage Message received from Cheryl Dean 3/29/2016 8:31:20 AM
My old roommate from Kent (was a witness at our wedding) is coming to sit with me at hospital.

iMessage Message sent by Judy 3/29/2016 8:32:00 AM
Beloved sis this is hard! I get anxious over minor procedures so I can only imagine how challenging this is. Praying for Gods peace to flood your heart and mind. Breathe in His great love, inhale the hope we have in Him! Breathe deeply in The Holy Spirit who is a deposit guaranteeing your inheritance. I love you so and wish I could be there with you!

iMessage Message received from Cheryl Dean 3/29/2016 8:35:34 AM

Thanks Sis. Satan is trying to put the memory in my mind of how awful the report was when docs came out after Ron's surgery.

iMessage Message sent by Judy 3/29/2016 8:35:55 AM
May you hear God's heartbeat of love as He shields you under His wing. May your friend support you marvelously! If I wasn't battling health issues I would be there.

iMessage Message received from Cheryl Dean 3/29/2016 8:36:48 AM
Danny and I have been strong together. My mind needs to be protected now that I'm alone. I hardly slept last night either.

iMessage Message sent by Judy 3/29/2016 8:40:52 AM
God is able to protect you. Do you have your Bible with you? It is so hard to read it when I am anxious but having it open and touching verses I have underlined remind me of his God has supplied what I needed. And how He made His presence known to me more deeply than ever before in that season. In our deepest valley, He is there.

iMessage Message sent by Judy 3/29/2016 8:43:53 AM
Praying for God to protect your mind...the peace that passes all understanding will guard your heart and mind in Christ Jesus. Thank you, Jesus, that you know my sister's suffering. You

know we are dust and struggle with fear. Cast
out the fear with your love Lord!

iMessage Message received from Cheryl Dean
3/29/2016 8:43:59 AM
In our deepest valley, He is deeper still. --Corrie
Ten Boom iM

iMessage Message sent by Judy 3/29/2016
8:45:44 AM
Yes! I have great confidence in that since 2001.
He met me in a way I have never gotten over and
will never forget!♥ love you so! Will continue
praying.

iMessage Message received from Cheryl Dean
3/29/2016 8:49:34 AM
Thank you for your testimony. Jesus is right by
my side and many angels have been dispatched
on our behalf

iMessage Message sent by Judy 3/29/2016
8:51:02 AM
Yes! He lives! And Jesus is praying for you...and
you know His prayers are answered.

Our friend, John Anderson, showed up to sit with me while I was in the waiting room. My pre-marriage, roomie, Kathryn Faudi, came to keep me company as well. We talked about nutrition, new medical inventions, the procedure Danny was having, and our own personal lives. Time ticked away as I watched the reader board. The five-hour mark came and went and still no word on Danny. I was so grateful to have friends with me so I didn't sit there wondering what could possibly be happening in the operating room. Friends and relatives began texting me for updates. This is when I came to the realization that one of my main jobs as caregiver was to be the communications officer for family and friends. I kept everyone in the loop. We continued to wait, and talk, and check the reader board. Kathryn, John, and I finally went out to lunch keeping my pager handy...still no word on Danny. I checked with the secretary to make sure my pager was working. She said it was working and called the surgery room to see how things were going. "They were finishing up," was her answer. John left for an appointment at this time. A word of advice here to caregivers: if someone volunteers to sit with you when your loved one is going through a surgery/procedure, say "Yes!" I thought I had wanted to just sit alone, read a book, enjoy the quietness after working with 7th and 8th graders. I am so thankful I had friends waiting with me, or my imagination would have filled my thoughts with all sorts of terrible scenarios! Having friends sit with me helped me stay calm.

Nine long hours later, Dr. Alseidi, took me into a consultation room, as Kathryn followed for support. I was trembling as the doctor filled us in on the surgery. Somewhere along the time-line of Danny's life, maybe due to the intensive gall bladder surgery years ago, Danny had developed adhesions and a lot of extra blood vessels. The doctor had great difficulty getting through these vessels and even had to reroute some of them. At this point the doctor could have given up and just closed Danny back up with the cancer still inside. He chose to move forward and give it his all. In the surgery, part of the pancreas, part of the duodenum (beginning of the small intestines), and part of the Ampullary duct were removed, along with the cancerous tumor. It was a grueling surgery but had been considered a success. The cancer had clear margins, an indicator that the cancer most likely had not spread. Later, I found out that this type of surgery was nearly the intensity of a liver transplant!

When I stepped into Danny's recovery room, he began singing, "I've got the joy, joy, joy, joy down in my heart!" He had an epidural in his back to help with the pain and a huge sutured area that looked like a frown to the observer but a smiley face from Danny's perspective. He had a blood pressure cuff on his arm, pulsating pressure socks on his calves to help prevent blood clots, IVs in his arms, a tube for pain meds, a tube for abdominal discharge, a CO_2 monitor in his nose, a urinary catheter, and a heart monitor. He had a big smile on his face though, and we thought the worst was behind us. I spent much of the evening texting and calling people about Danny's surgery.

I was allowed to sleep in his room and I had a relatively comfortable bed to sleep on. Throughout the night, we were awakened to various beeps and alarms. Nurses came in often to check Danny's stats and condition. Every few hours, he was given a Heparin shot to help prevent clots. The shot itself didn't hurt, but as the solution was pushed into his system, it was excruciating to Danny. He came to dread the shot.

In the early morning, I woke up to the nurses scurrying around, attempting to bring down the horrible acid reflux Danny was having. His blood pressure went way down, he got very dizzy and he almost passed out. He was already taking medicine for acid reflux so it was normally under control, but the intensity of it now was off the charts. I sat watching the flurry of activity and prayed for Danny to be leveled out. For some reason, Danny also had a fever.

Some friends, Melvin and Becky Hoage, stopped in to see us that evening. While we all laid hands on Danny and prayed for him, I felt a hand on my shoulder. When I opened my eyes, I discovered it was the hand of a nurse who had been praying with us. Melvin kept us in stitches and Danny nearly popped his own stitches! Melvin and Becky gave Danny a comfy, gray blanket with Quinault pattern on it because Melvin is from the Quinault tribe. They also gave Danny a hand-carved Native American paddle. "It's for your journey ahead," Melvin said. God had told both Danny and me that we would get through this. Little did we know how long the "this" would be. We definitely had a journey ahead.

Grant and Lauri Russell came by to visit and filled the room with laughter. Following the advice of friends that I rest up and take time for myself so I could be strong for the journey, I slept in the

Baroness Hotel that night. It was a hotel built in the 1930s, reminiscent of the Great Gatsby era but was semi-remodeled with furniture from the 70s. Because the room I was scheduled for was having refrigerator problems and I needed a refrigerator for my RA medicine, the hotel upgraded me to a queen size suite. Thank you, God, for favor! I relaxed just by myself, calmly thinking the worst was behind us. I slept like a baby but woke up in a panic when I realized I had forgotten to feed the $25 a day parking meter. When I got to the parking lot, a ticket for $84 was on my windshield. Ouch! Didn't the parking lot company realize my husband was in the hospital, and besides…I'm a daughter of the Most High King! (This is something I am really trying to gasp myself.) I sent an email to the parking lot company telling my circumstances and how my mind wasn't on the parking meter. I didn't mention the part about being a daughter of the King, but I did ask for mercy and prayed God would move their hearts. With all our expenses lately, I certainly didn't need an extra one.

When I got to Danny's room, nurses were trying to get him to sit up, but he was too dizzy and his blood pressure kept plummeting. The GERD was not as bad as the day before but he was still dealing with it. He had another CT scan to see how all the pieced together organs were doing and to see why he was having a low-grade fever. Everything checked out fine.

My daughter's mother-in-law, Laurinda Steele, stopped by with her boyfriend, Ernie. She came bearing gifts: a specialty cupcake, a key to her house where I would be able to shower and sleep from Sunday night till we were discharged, and a sweet get-well card from my grandchildren with real band aids stuck to it. Melvin stopped by and brought a CD player and the Bible on tape. Since we had lived near Seattle before moving to Yakima, we had old friends who could visit us while we were "visiting" Seattle. Danny was super groggy so I stepped outside to get some rare Seattle sunshine in the hotel parking lot and texted our myriad of Danny update followers. I was feeling like things were on the upswing but still felt headachy.

Here's a word of encouragement from my sis via text:

iMessage Message sent by Judy 3/31/2016 3:56:59 PM
I am so proud of you Sis! You walk through these things with such great faith! It encourages me to trust God!

iMessage Message received from Cheryl Dean 3/31/2016 3:58:26 PM
That's the best way to get through things!

iMessage Message from Judy sent 3/31/2016 3:59:14 PM
Some of us go kicking and screaming...ahem!

iMessage Message from Judy sent 3/31/2016 3:59:38 PM
Glad God saved us so we can live life with Him!

**iMessage Message received from Cheryl Dean 3/31/2016 4:13:02 PM
I would sure be a different person without Him. Danny and I decided to Free Fall with God -- following him at all cost; resting with him in peace. Danny is better at this!**

The nurses took out Danny's catheter—owie! One tube down. He still had a tube for pain meds, a tube for his stomach discharge, a heart monitor, CO2 monitor coming out of his nose, and an epidural tube out of his back. I got to take a look at Danny's Frankenstein-ish stitches which curved across his abdomen like a railroad track.

Friday, April 1 The next morning as I awoke in my hotel room, I could sure tell I wasn't in Yakima anymore as I looked out the window to an old, brick apartment complex a yard or two away. I sat down to my breakfast of coffee and instant oatmeal at the dinette, and then remembered to feed the parking meter. Feeding the meter became one of my big jobs during our hospital stay.

I arrived at Danny's room and found him missing me horribly. Since he's my strong guy who I usually depend on, it was strange to have switched roles. The doctors had taken out the epidural and were now administering oral meds. Danny began to feel pain in his abdomen which had escalated to a 7. He had to wait another hour for the next dose of pain meds. Suddenly, his pain escalated to a 10+. Danny was in so much pain, he couldn't even take a call from one of his best friends, Jesse Ball. My poor baby was wrapped in heated hospital blankets along with the Quinault blanket, and had tubes coming out of body as he moaned. He was not singing anymore.

His daughter, Arielle, from Portland, and his daughter, Naomi, (who currently lives with us) were due to arrive at 1:00. Before the evening was out, Danny was stable enough to be moved off the critical care unit to the 15th floor. With Danny safely tucked in to his new room, Naomi, Arielle, and I walked to dinner at Vito's Restaurant. It was extremely dark in the restaurant, we could barely see our table, and it looked like a Mafia meeting place. One of the old 1960's pictures displayed near a meeting room even showed a group of people eating with a gun on the table! With all the current stressors, it was nice to encounter interesting things to take our mind off reality.

Steve and Tina McCorkle visited Danny while we were at dinner. Danny's pain escalated to a 10+ again. As he cried out in pain he declared, "Jesus, You are worthy of praise!" Tina and Steve said they had never experienced such an intensity of worship in their lives before. Immediately, the new nurse rushed in and gave Danny a different, super strong pain med. Thank you to one of our favorite nurses, Becky.

Saturday, April 2 Danny was heavily drugged with pain meds since he had such difficulty the day before. At one point, he woke up and told me, "As you take up your weapons of war to fight the enemy, you're a Minuteman...." Then he faded out again. According to Wikipedia (please don't tell my students I used Wikipedia as a resource!):

"**Minutemen** were civilian colonists who independently organized to form well-prepared militia companies self-trained in weaponry, tactics, and military strategies from the American colonial partisan militia during the American Revolutionary War. They were also known for being ready in a minute's notice. They provided a highly mobile, rapidly deployed force that allowed the colonies to respond immediately to war threats, hence the name."

I think there is something prophetic in that.

For a while, Danny had the TV channel on an old 50s movie he really didn't seem to be watching. "This is so droll," he commented. Then his eyes rolled up into the back of his head and he went back to sleep. It was funny that he would still use big words even when he was sedated but it was concerning seeing him drugged out. I was just relieved he wasn't in pain—it's so hard to watch your loved one in pain. Doctors continued to run tests to see what could be causing the blood in his discharge tube/bag and did a sonogram on him to check his bladder input. Danny continued to be poked for blood-work checks.

I walked to a local pharmacy with Naomi for snacks, something to help me sleep, and pain meds. I had been having intense pelvic pain and was hoping I wouldn't have to see a doctor myself. I just didn't have time to be sick. Naomi, Arielle, and I were sharing a room at the Baroness Hotel. We contemplated why there would be bars on the windows of our 5th floor room when it wouldn't be possible for someone to break in. We finally deduced the bars were to keep the Puget Sound seagulls out. Every time we rode the hotel's 1930s elevator, we wondered if we would one day get stuck in it.

Praise God and thank you to the parking company. They showed us mercy by removing the extra late charge on my parking fee!

Our dear friend, Dr. Bruce Cook came for a long visit with Danny and me while our daughters went to the hotel room to watch a movie. When Bruce and Danny began to talk about business and Kingdom things, Danny was enlivened and eloquent. I hadn't seen him like this since we had been in the hospital.

I left them alone and went for a walk in the sunshine. I kept reminding myself to take care of myself as others had advised and leaving Danny's side was nothing to feel guilty about. Everywhere I looked, I saw signs advertising the hospital which said, "Be remarkable." The Lord was trying to tell me something, I thought. The Holy Spirit quietly said, "Write. Be remarkable."

Back at the room, Bruce prayed over both of us and prophesied that the Lord had said that I should write, like He has told me before. He said I don't need any more encouragement to do it—just do it. This was spot-on since I had just earlier heard the Lord tell me to write.

Sunday, April 3 The hospital was strangely quiet since it was the weekend. Danny had dreamed about waking up in the hospital. In the dream, someone was going through something even more intense than he was experiencing and it was affecting the whole nation of England. (I thought this was especially interesting since Danny had hallucinated about Minute-men from the Revolutionary War before and was now talking about England.) The physical therapist tried to get him up and walking (a pre-requisite to leaving the hospital) but he was still very dizzy. He was trying so hard! Eventually he was able to take several walks as long as one person pushed his IV pole and another person followed along with a chair he could collapse into when needed.

Naomi and Arielle visited with their dad while I took my luggage to Laurinda's condo so I could find her home while it was still light. Driving through the crazy, touristy traffic of Seattle was still a challenge for me. I stopped in at Whole Foods which had to be reached from the underground parking structure—only in Seattle. After missing Magnolia and ending up in Ballard, and after many bumps and bruises trying to get my luggage up the elevator to Laurinda's condo, I arrived back at Danny's hospital room and discovered I had missed the second visit by the McCorkels. Arielle and

Naomi headed home. On the way in to the hospital, I saw Carrie Corey who had been visiting Danny with her husband. A while later, Ruth and Ken Marshall and Dave Norman (friends we had ministered with at Tacoma First Nations Gathering—a Native American group) came to visit. This visit involved trying to get a wheelchair for Ruth who had just had surgery herself. Since it was the weekend, the sliding doors locked behind me. We didn't want to push a wheel chair up the steep street to get to another entrance so surprisingly, Ken was able to pry the hospital sliding doors open so we could get back into the hospital entrance. Then we wound through the empty part of the hospital taking two different elevators to get to Danny's room. I'm sure there is a security camera video tape with this ragtag group sneaking through the closed part of the hospital. Since Virginia Mason was built on a hill, getting around the hospital was quite an adventure. Since I was at the hospital for so long, I became a "tour guide" for others who got lost. Danny and I were so thankful for all those who visited. They cheered him up and kept me occupied. I apologize if, in my spotty memory, I missed mentioning any of the visitors who took the time to visit us.

After scarfing down a veggie burger at the cafeteria—I was starting to be a regular there and began to have daily chats with the food service people—I returned to the hospital room and watched a Final Four Women's basketball game with Danny. One of my old students from Seattle Christian School was playing for University of

Washington. Katie Collier was a spectacular basketball player and had overcome blood cancer while she was in high school. After the game, which UW sadly lost, I drove through Seattle, past the Space Needle, and on to Magnolia where I did laundry, took a shower, and relaxed at Laurinda's condo. This was the fifth place I had stayed in for the past seven days. Other friends had offered to put me up too, but I didn't want to get too far away from my precious patient.

Monday, April 4 This week was Spring Break from school so I didn't have to be concerned using up my sick days and I didn't have to email sub plans to the school. I was a little nervous about the condition of my classroom and students since they had a couple different subs that previous week. Before I left Laurinda's home, I face-timed with my daughter, Jackie, and the grandkids, Luke and Ellie. Two-year-old Ellie ran off with the phone and put it in a closet in her room. Before I knew it, she had closed the door with "me" still in there. "Help!" I called out. "Grandma is stuck in the closet!" It was nice, in the middle of the hospital stress, to have a diversion.

I was met with good news when I arrived at the hospital. The dizziness was gone and Danny was able to walk more. We were going home tomorrow!!! I say "we," even though Danny was the only patient, because "we" were in the ordeal/adventure together. Even though I wasn't bedridden, in pain and on meds, or poked and prodded every 15 minutes, I was still in this. I was the communications officer, urinal retriever, snack getter, doctor and nurse liaison, stool monitor, thermostat changer, drink pourer, visitor scheduler, advocate, and encourager. We were in this together.

Danny's dizziness was gone, he was walking a bit more, and he had had a bowel movement. I discovered that how Danny's bowels functioned was extremely important to the hospital and we all had to closely monitor it. We newlyweds were becoming more intimately involved than we thought possible. Bowel movements were now a cause for celebration.

Danny seemed so drained, not his usual talkative self. He wasn't even that enthusiastic about March Madness and the Final Four basketball games. I was praying constantly. I know we should be doing that anyway, but sickness has a way of bringing us to our knees more often. Bruce Cook brought us some healthy Sozo drinks and Recovery water (oxygenated healing water). I walked to a McDonalds to get Danny a cheeseburger, at his request—not a healing contribution, but I was glad to at least see him eat part of it.

After Danny started dozing, I hiked down steep 9th Avenue to the Seattle Public Library where Shakespeare's First and Third Folios were on display for a short period of time. The First Folio was the first collection of many of Shakespeare's plays (Macbeth, Hamlet etc.). The playwright's plays would have dissolved into oblivion if these plays had not been published by two of

Shakespeare's acting friends in 1623 (7 years after the Bard's death). Since I had taught several of Shakespeare's plays in my high school classes, I was beyond excited to see the exhibit and so thankful that it was in town at just the right week for me to see it. Luckily, the armed guard next to the glass display case didn't have to restrain my zeal as I excitedly looked at the manuscripts. I made up for all the hours of sitting around in the hospital as I broke into a sweat hiking back up the steep hill to Virginia Mason. Thank you for the diversion from the hospital, God.

That afternoon, Dr. Rose, the intern/doctor, came in to discuss the results of Danny's tests—every tissue sample they had removed from Danny's abdomen and lymph nodes came back cancer free. Hallelujah—thank you Jesus!! Grant Russell and Bruce Cook called Danny that night. KCIA, Kingdom Congressional International Alliance, (the business group Danny and I are a part of and Bruce is the president) sent flowers with a stuffed penguin (which Danny collects). The properly named Sunshine Committee from my school, Lewis and Clark Middle School, sent Danny a flower arrangement too. Danny lifted his hand off the bed, held my hand, and said, "I just want to go to sleep so I can wake up tomorrow and go home." We thought the worst was over and had no idea of the travail ahead.

Chapter 5

The Winding Road to Recovery – Cheryl

"But when I am afraid, I will put my confidence in you." (Psalm 56:3 Living Bible)

"For you have saved me from death and my feet from slipping, so that I can walk before the Lord in the land of the living." (Psalm 56:13 Living Bible)

Tuesday, April 5 When I arrived in Danny's room after spending the night at Laurinda's house, he was so ready to get out of the hospital. His eyes were panicked and he said, "I have to get out of here now!" We had an hour wait getting Danny's meds from the pharmacy. Eventually transport took Danny to the surgery entrance in a wheelchair.

By the time we drove the 2 ½ hours home, Danny was pathetic and weak. He was in pain and had no appetite. We had no chair for him to sit on in the shower so I got the idea to wash up the plastic lawn chair side-table to use. Since Danny had only had sponge baths in his week-long stay in the hospital, he felt human again to have a full shower. We stayed up till midnight just being together (without having nurses around to check vitals) while we watched Gregory Peck in *The Guns of Navarrone*.

Wednesday, April 6 Last night, Danny was too week to get up the stairs to our bedroom so he slept downstairs. I slept upstairs so I wouldn't disturb him. He texted me at 2 am and 6 am needing meds and comfort. Throughout the day, I kept a chart of Danny's medicine regime and gave him the meds throughout the day. He is down to 190 pounds and is not eating anything.

Thursday, April 7 I shopped for a variety of foods to try to perk Danny's appetite. Danny and I were watching TV together when he suddenly got violently sick—he was super-hot, threw up, had stomach cramps, and bouts of diarrhea. I was concerned but we assumed it was a part of post-surgery healing.

Friday, April 8 It was a really hot day and air conditioning wars began. Danny was weak and rapidly losing weight so he was cold all the time while the rest of us were boiling. While Danny's friend Paul visited him, I went to the grocery store to forage for food that Danny might finally eat. I had tried so many foods already, as well as made decisions about other things. I felt overwhelmed and stressed. Danny was sitting up more and moving about better on his own today. While we had been in the hospital, our yard had turned into a two-foot weed farm so we had our lawn guy mow the lawn—a money extravagance for us. It had only been a week-and-a-half from Danny's surgery, but I was already feeling frustration from giving so much care and not being able to find ways to make him happy. He didn't want to listen to music or watch TV or even read. I finally convinced him to listen to some soaking music. He hadn't been reading anything even his Bible which he usually loves to read every day. We had minimal conversations and Danny wasn't his usual self: talkative, profound, smiley, fun, a decision maker. I cooked a chicken with artichoke sauce in the crockpot all day and it made him nauseous. Naomi and I enjoyed the meal while Danny could hardly get a bite down. We were finally able to watch the latest Star Wars movie with Naomi. Danny was beginning to back off his pain meds.

Saturday, April 9 Danny didn't text me at all during the night or morning. I went down about 7:45 am and found him peacefully sleeping on the red, velour love seat in the prayer room. Danny had gone all night without pain meds so I had the hope that he was on the mend.

That morning, we watched the Azusa Now Conference live from Los Angeles. It was a great encouragement to watch reconciliation with people groups and see people so immersed in worship together. Pastor Shawn Niles, a master chef and caterer on the side, prepared and brought over flank steak tacos, with cilantro pears on top. It was delicious and Danny actually ate a whole taco. We thought Shawn had broken the inability to eat issue. We continued to watch Azusa Now and Danny remarked that, "This is what I really needed." "Praise you Jesus—help Danny recover quickly," I prayed.

I wrote this in my journal: "Danny ate some peach baby food this morning. He hasn't wanted to eat much of anything and has lost so much weight. He hasn't wanted to listen to much music, just a little

Deeper Still

TV.... He hasn't been his usual self of reading the Word every morning before he gets out of bed. He hasn't talked much about the Lord or anything lately. [Anybody who knows Danny, knows he loves to talk.] He mostly sits quietly or naps. This is all to be expected, but it feels weird, worrisome, concerning. It is all hitting me harder than I thought it would. This doesn't seem like my husband. I know it has only been two weeks and surgery takes a lot out of a person, especially when you lose part of your pancreas and duodenum—it interferes with normal eating—but it's hard to see him so weak. Usually, I depend on him to be the strong one. He seems lethargic and emotionally despondent. I'm feeling despondent. I miss the normal Danny. I miss our conversations. I miss his strong embrace."

Before Danny got ill, he was at a point in his life where he was really walking in his gifts. We had a large weekly home group, he had been teaching a Bible class on Saturdays, and was beginning to be used in our church. What we were going through was a major setback.

In the evenings, Danny would have severe abdominal pain, hot flashes, and then began to vomit violently and had diarrhea. The doctor-prescribed anti-nausea medicine did not seem to be helping. We assumed this was just a natural part of the healing process but were still concerned.

Tuesday April 12, I began watching a video series on my computer called, *The Truth About Cancer*, by

Ty Bollinger. In the series, Ty interviews many doctors, nutritionists, and cancer survivors. It was so informative and timely. Judy watched it at the same time and we texted each other back and forth about ideas we gleaned from each episode. We were excited to hear about alternatives to chemotherapy and its devastating effects. Throughout the days ahead of emergency runs and recovery, I squeezed in the episodes learning more and more. This series gave me the relief that cancer didn't mean a death sentence.

Friday, April 15 We went to Virginia Mason in Seattle for a post-surgery checkup with Dr. Alseidi. Danny had been feverish off and on, but had decided to wait till his checkup to see what that was all about. The doctors ran a CT scan and discovered Danny had an infection in his abdomen. We were immediately admitted to the hospital so that Danny could be treated with antibiotics and get a drainage bag put into his side. Since the hospital stay was totally unexpected, we hadn't brought any overnight stuff with us. The doctor requested the 18th oncology floor for our stay because it had the better, quieter rooms and, it turns out, the best views of Seattle and Puget Sound. We qualified for that particular floor since Danny was being treated for cancer. As soon as we were nestled in our room, the search for overnight supplies began--mobile phone charger, toothbrushes, etc. We ended up needing to stay for a few days so Naomi (who was back in Yakima) met Laurinda (my daughter's mom in law) to hand off some clothes, makeup and meds for me.

Danny was fine with his low maintenance, "back door cooling vent" hospital gown.

While I was at the hospital, I diligently watched the video series, *The Cure for Cancer*. One thing I had learned about in these videos was the use of Frankincense for the shrinkage and dissolving of tumors. Fortunately, I went to Laurinda's essential oil party on Sunday and learned more about what oils could do and was finally able to take a shower which I hadn't had in a few days. (Certain parts of the hospital weren't keen on the idea of visitors using the patient's shower/bathroom.) I was on a mission to learn more about fighting cancer with nutrition because I didn't want that "bad boy" to return. I had already lost my brother and grandfather to cancer and had some minor cancer removed from my shin; I didn't want cancer to have any hold on my family. I had already been on a search for relief from rheumatoid arthritis through nutrition and now began to diligently apply Frankincense to where the skin cancer had been.

iMessage Message sent by Judy 4/16/2016 8:47:03 AM
He who dwells in the shelter of the Most High will abide in the shadow of the Almighty. I will say to the Lord, "my refuge and my fortress, my God, in whom I trust." For he will deliver you from the snare of the Fowler and from the deadly pestilence. He will cover you with his pinions and under his wings you will find refuge; his faithfulness is a shield and buckler. Psalm

91:1-4. Your morning reminder of our glorious God who is our Redeemer and Rescuer!

iMessage Message received from Cheryl Dean 4/16/2016 8:54:22 AM
Wonderful verse. I dreamed that I brought Danny to Jesus. Jesus put his hand on Danny's abdomen and was healing him. I was on my knees in grief and Jesus dispatched an angel to comfort me.

iMessage Message received from Cheryl Dean 4/16/2016 8:55:25 AM
Danny will get the tubes in this morning. He is already feeling better having the IV antibiotics overnight and white blood cell count is going down.

iMessage Message sent by Judy 4/16/2016 8:55:54 AM
Beautiful picture of Christ's comfort! I love you Sis. How is Danny? I need to apologize too! I sent a care package to Danny but realized after watching the video last night that I sent him poison in that box. There are some sugar foods in there. Please forgive me. [By watching *The Cure for Cancer*, Judy and I were learning how sugar feeds cancer.]

iMessage Message received from Cheryl Dean 4/16/2016 8:57:11 AM
Don't worry about it did. I'll eat it. One last hurrah.

We stayed in the hospital for two more days so the hospital could monitor the infection and drain bag. I had wondered why the payment for our hotel wasn't showing up on our credit card.

iMessage Message received from Cheryl Dean 4/18/2016 1:56:38 PM
Yesterday I went to the hotel I had stayed in the last time we were here to see why they hadn't taken out the charge yet. It turns out a friend had paid for it!!!!!

iMessage Message sent by Judy 4/18/2016 1:57:06 PM
How wonderful! God is good!

iMessage Message sent by Judy 4/18/2016 2:02:46 PM
He is good all the time; this is just one of many evidences of His kindness expressed through the body of Christ!

Monday, April 18 My son Josh and his beautiful wife, Alisa, came by the hospital to take me to dinner. They live in Tacoma which is an hour away. We walked to a nearby Thai restaurant—I was getting to know my way around Seattle by now and we had a fun time of fellowship.

Danny and I were able to come home on Sunday with only one school day missed. For the next two weeks, Naomi and I took turns draining Danny's infection bag and flushing the drain tube. It was so hard to not gag while we unhooked the bag, flushed the tube in his side with a saline syringe, and reconnected the tube to the bag. While I was teaching during the day, Naomi would take on the duties. We were becoming quite the nurses.

One night, I woke up to find my back was soaking wet. At first, I thought I had had a post-menopausal hot flash but doubted I would be that wet. Then a horrifying thought hit me that Danny's drain had leaked and I was lying in infectious goop! I froze in fear. "Danny, I think you leaked; turn the light on quick." He got out of bed and checked all the tubing while I lay there wet, thinking, "Oooooh Ick! I'm going to have to take a shower at two in the morning!" That's when it dawned on Danny that he had fallen asleep with a cup of water in his hand. The cup must have fallen out of his hand while he slept and the water poured out on me. Whew!! I was so relieved and we had a good laugh.

April 29 We went to Seattle for Danny's checkup hoping the drainage tube/bag would be taken out. Instead, the doctor put in a larger tube because he didn't think the infection was draining sufficiently. Fortunately, the procedure did not involve an overnight stay in the hospital. Now Danny was in more pain than before and his fluid bag had more blood in it. I tried so hard to not gag in front of him when I changed it.

"I have set the Lord continually before me; because He is at my right hand, I will not be shaken."
(Psalm 16:8 Living Bible)

Sunday, May 1 Since my son, Josh, was graduating from Northwest Christian University in Kirkland on Mother's Day weekend, my daughters decided to celebrate Mother's Day early. Jackie's family was visiting from Star, Idaho and accompanied me to church that morning while Danny stayed home. It was one of the first times he had been left alone and he said he could handle it. When we got home, Danny was feeling puny with flu like symptoms he had had off and on after surgery. Jackie started making turkey sliders for lunch and my other daughter, Shannon, was on her way from Kittitas, WA (40 minutes from Yakima) with her husband, Shane, and the boys, Dylan, Lincoln, and Warner to celebrate with us.

Jackie's four-year-old, Luke, came into the bedroom and said "hi" to Danny but hung back when he saw how sickly he looked. We ushered Luke out when Danny started getting stomach cramps. I was up and down the stairs watching the kids and letting Jackie know how Danny was doing, then back up the stairs to check on Danny. Dark blood was showing up in Danny's drain bag and Danny had passed blood in the toilet. I started thinking I should get Danny to the emergency room, but was going to wait until my son-in-law, Shane, showed up to help me get Danny down the stairs.

Right when I heard Shannon and her family arrive, Danny felt violently ill so I helped him to the bathroom. He passed more blood in the toilet and then collapsed onto the floor, weak and trembling. I hadn't realized how skinny Danny had become and was shocked. I cleaned Danny up and covered him with a blanket. While I was trying to figure out how I could possibly get his 6' 2" frame into the bed, Danny mustered enough strength to pull himself up on his knees and crawl to the bed. I knew Shane and I would never be able to get him out to the car. That's when I made the first 911 call of my life. My daughters and Shane scurried around collecting grandkids to take them to the park so they wouldn't have to see Grandpa taken away in an ambulance.

Firemen got to our house in minutes. They started taking vitals on Danny who now looked grayish-white. His insulin count was off. Then the paramedics arrived and looked Danny over while they asked questions. Our bedroom was filled with calm, efficient men. Because our stairs are an L shape, it was impossible to get a stretcher down the stairs. The medics brought up a heavy dining room chair to use. As they lifted Danny onto the chair, he yelled out in pain, his head dropped, and he looked like he was about to pass out. This is when I started feeling panicky. I had been relatively calm and proactive until that point. I followed as the medics maneuvered Danny down the stairs and into the ambulance. As the ambulance zipped away with my precious cargo, I called my daughters to tell them they could bring the kids back. I called Naomi who was out shopping and told her to meet us at the hospital. By the time I got to the Memorial Hospital, Naomi and Pastor Shawn were already waiting there.

There was a hubbub of medical activity around Danny—warming blankets were put on him, vitals taken, blood drawn. The doctor determined he had lost so much blood that he needed a transfusion. We agreed was a good idea. That's when they gave us a consent form to sign saying we were aware of the minute chance that Aids or Hepatitis could be in the blood. I felt hesitant about that point but knew he needed blood to survive. Shawn prayed, "Lord, keep this blood covered by your blood." As the lifeblood flowed into Danny's veins, he began to look healthier.

Doctors gave Danny a CT scan and contemplated giving him an endoscopy (down the throat to the stomach) to see what was going on. They called Virginia Mason Hospital and determined that Danny should be taken there because they knew his surgery and drain tube details. This was to be Danny's second ride in an ambulance to Seattle. I teased Danny that his first ambulance ride wasn't enough for him; he had to go for two. I rushed home, ate one of Jackie's slider sandwiches while I filled her in on what was happening, and then packed for the trip to Seattle. Not wanting to fall asleep at the wheel, I grabbed a Mountain Dew, then drove over Snoqualmie Pass and made it to Seattle by 12:45 AM.

This time, we got a room on the 15th floor. It was a smaller room but had a fantastic view of the Seattle lights with Lake Washington in the background. The view brought me joy--I was looking for anything joyful in the moment at this point. The nurses squeezed a folding bed for me next to Danny's bed. The first night, the mattress coils gouged me and even bruised my delicate skin (caused by RA meds over the years). I was so thankful that my husband was still alive; I figured I could put up with a bed of nails for a night. The next morning, I got another mattress and put it on top of the bed of nails. I was quite comfortable now.

Naomi drove over from Yakima to visit. Arielle and her husband, Chris, drove up from Portland. Later, Naomi picked up Danny's other daughter Bethany from the train station. This was an answer to my prayers of reconciliation for Danny and his daughter.

Danny had been scheduled to do an angiogram the next morning, May 3rd. The "kids" (young adults really) stayed in a hotel. The next morning, Danny was taken down for the procedure to check on internal bleeding. We sat in the waiting room with a pager while Danny's son Caleb was on his way to visit his father. This was another answer to my prayer for reconciliation. While Danny waited in his prep room, we visited him one at a time. Bethany and her dad resolved some long-standing hurts in their sweet time together. Meanwhile, I had to continue to make lesson plans for my substitute teacher and email them to my school office.

When I went to see Danny after the procedure, he was pretty out of it; his eyes were rolling up in his head and he asked about the purple men who had helped him. I thought, "Uh oh, that is some strong stuff they gave him." Later I learned that sometimes the respiration department wears purple scrubs. Maybe Danny wasn't imagining things after all. The radiologist who had performed the angiogram exploration decided that there was an aneurysm in Danny's working artery and the other artery was blocked. One of the arteries was compensating for the other. He recommended that Danny have an angiogram again when he had rest from all the radiation of the first angiogram. On Thursday, they would put a stent in the plugged artery and plug up the branch of the artery with the aneurysm/leak. One of the nurses' assistants or CPTs (Certified Patient Technician) we had during this hospital stay was named, "ThankGod." Seriously. He was from Nigeria where parents often gave their children those kinds of names. We loved the name and were so encouraged when ThankGod started quoting scriptures to us.

John Anderson visited that evening and gave Danny and me hugs and encouragement. It was 8:00 by this time and I hadn't eaten all day so I walked outside to the Rhododendron Café where I cried as I ate my turkey sandwich. I was feeling so many emotions as I reflected on the day: relieved that something was going to be done for Danny, stressed that we found ourselves once again in the hospital, exhausted from keeping family and friends in the loop about Danny's condition, and overwhelmed with all the family interactions. Danny and I had only been married for three years, so our blended family was still getting used to each other and here we were going through trauma together. The waiter comforted me as I tried to drape my hair over my tear streaked cheeks. I didn't want to concern the other patrons. I was a pathetic mess.

Thursday, May 5 Danny's surgeon had talked to the radiologist and told him he had already noticed the blocked artery during surgery. The blockage probably had been there for probably years so the other artery was taking over just fine. The aneurysm was probably a stump from a previous gall bladder removal surgery; the bleeding was most likely from the infection drainage tube. So, the drainage tube was removed, much to our joy. Danny was so glad to get rid of that painful thing. I was glad to know he would be out of pain and I wouldn't have to drain that tube anymore. We got to go home that day and found our roses were in bloom. Life was going on around us even though Danny's life was precarious.

Chapter 6

Life Flight – Cheryl

Friday, May 6 It was difficult to return to the classroom amidst so much trauma, but it was nice to finally be back in a routine. The staff was caring and many said they had been praying. Some co-workers were afraid to ask how things were with Danny because they were afraid it could be bad news and hard for me to talk. I sent an email around to inform everyone what was happening and thank them for their continued prayer and support. I sent texts, Facebook messages, and phone call updates to relatives. I was getting efficient at copying and pasting messages to family and friends and was thankful I had Facebook as a vehicle to broadcast updates and prayer requests. My big concern now was Danny was getting so skinny he looked like a malnourished person from a concentration camp!

My son's graduation from Northwest University in Kirkland was the next day so I planned the drive over the pass once again and leaving Danny in the care of Naomi. I started packing and then jumped in the shower.

Suddenly, I heard Naomi yell, "You'd better get out here!"

I ran out of the bathroom, soaking wet with a towel wrapped around me and my wet hair in disarray. Danny had just thrown up blood into a dish-tub. I asked Danny how he was doing then threw on some clothes while Naomi called 911. Naomi had dumped the first issue of blood down the toilet but when Danny threw up again I decided to keep it to show the medics. Within minutes the medics were there.

"Hello Mr. Dean. You are looking better this time." They proceeded to ask me what had happened and asked me to refresh their memory on the case. Two other strapping EMTs ran downstairs for the dining room chair to carry Danny down the awkward, twisty staircase. As Danny was sitting up in the chair, he threw up a massive amount of red blood with huge clots into the dish-tub he had in his lap.

One clot looked like a tube and, and another the size of a golf club. in my state of mind, I thought he had thrown up an intestine. The EMT reassured me it couldn't be. I was relatively calm as I moved around with a pink medical tub full of my husband's blood asking, "Look at this. Is this okay?" It was surreal, like I was watching the events unfold-not like I was there in person. Now I realize that I was in shock. Even now, I can barely talk about that day because it was so horrific. But I need to talk about it. If I bury it, the trauma will stay with me. Danny was once again taken away by ambulance. I somehow found the wherewithal to dry my hair and crazily finish packing. Now I was packing, not because I was going to my son's graduation, but because I would once again be staying in the hospital.

Deeper Still

By the time I got to the emergency room at Memorial Hospital in Yakima, my good friend from home-group, Stephanie Reiland, was already there. Danny wasn't in a room yet so we weren't allowed to go back and see him. Stephanie and I were sitting in the waiting room, holding hands, when Paul and Beth Stadler arrived. They were all such a big comfort. When I finally was allowed into Danny's room I almost collapsed at the sight. He was totally wrapped in the silver warming blankets and was ashen colored. He looked utterly pathetic and deathly ill. Our friends came in separately to pray over him and were also shocked at the sight.

Danny weakly asked for a bedpan which I had to awkwardly position under his bottom. The nurse was calmly but swiftly adjusting monitors. Danny was hooked up for another infusion of blood. Doctor Hutchinson decided it would be best to airlift Danny to Virginia Mason in Seattle again. I asked the doctor if he made this decision because Danny was receiving a blood transfusion and the ambulance wouldn't transport patients being transfused or if it was because of the urgency of the situation. He said, "It's urgent."

I kissed Danny, told him I loved him, then said I was going to get a head start and drive to Seattle and meet him there. It was now after midnight, only one day after we had returned from our last hospital run. Fortunately, I already had my suitcase in the car and only had to make a quick stop for some caffeine to keep me awake for the drive ahead. Since it was so late at night, the roads were clear except for some construction projects. It was pitch black and scary going around some of the mountainous curves especially because I was pushing the speed limit. Lord, forgive me.

I experienced so much emotion in this two-and-a-half-hour drive. I turned on a Christian station with encouraging songs and sang along loudly as I tried to focus on my mission of reaching the hospital. I even made up songs about God's greatness and Danny's healing. Suddenly, the seriousness of the situation and the possibility of Danny's death speared me through the heart. I grieved, I cried, and I contended. I wailed in intercession, "Lord, you told me Danny would get through this! You are the God who keeps His word." My heart was once again calmed with His promise.

I saw a bright star as I drove. Towering pine trees would hide the star and then it would once again reveal itself. It seemed as if the star was guiding me and reassuring me. Then I envisioned the star as Danny's helicopter life flight. I imagined that I was following his helicopter to the hospital and as long as I saw the star, I knew he was still alive.

I arrived at Virginia Mason at 3:00 in the morning. The security guard was gracious enough to follow me to the parking garage and drive me back to the emergency room. I choked on the words when I asked the desk clerk about Danny Dean, praying my husband was still alive. She opened the security door and gave me his room number. I breathed a sigh of relief knowing this meant he was still alive.

Danny was in a sterile room and hooked up to another blood transfusion, saline solution, and pain meds bags. He weakly said, "Hi," as I held his hand.

There were no reclining chairs available so I had to try to sleep on a folding chair. I cuddled up with the Quinault blanket, our traveling companion, and sat on the metal chair by Danny's bed. I struggled for several hours and could not get comfortable enough to sleep. I was so tired and had been under such stress; I just held a pillow against my chest to hold my head up and cried in anguish. My consolation was being able to hear Danny snore in his bed next to me—the nicest sound in the world at this moment.

About 9 am we finally got a room on the 18th floor. Our room was big and had a folding couch for me to sleep on but the view was an ugly spot of the back of a building. I was feeling claustrophobic so my sister once again encouraged me.

iMessage Message sent by Judy 5/7/2016 7:54:20 AM
You guys have been through such a rough stretch; my heart aches. I am crying out to God for you.

iMessage Message received from Cheryl Dean 5/7/2016 7:55:58 AM
Thank you, Judy, we are going through the wringer. Danny is feeling better now.

iMessage Message sent by Judy 5/7/2016 7:57:11 AM
Praise God for mercy!

iMessage Message received from Cheryl Dean 5/7/2016 8:19:05 AM
Claustrophobic room. Judy, I feel panicky. I think it's the lack of sleep. I had a mini panic attack Thursday night.

iMessage Message sent by Judy 5/7/2016 8:21:04 AM
You are going through a difficult time with a capital D. Practice slow breathing, in through your nose out through your mouth and focus on how slow you can get it. Can you run over to Laurinda's place to sleep while Danny goes through the endoscopy?

iMessage Message sent by Judy 5/7/2016 8:38:43 AM
Sleep deprivation also leads to panicky feelings...as you get some rest those will fade. And you have endured weeks of stress which take a toll. Praying for peace and sleep for you.

This was by far the scariest visit because Danny seemed so close to death. He received five bags of blood and one bag of plasma. He was hooked up to a saline IV. A port was put in his arm so he could get nutrition-- it looked more like the nurses were feeding him Mountain Dew.

As I finally I lay down to rest, my daughters sent me texts and pictures of Josh's graduation. I was so sad to miss it but at least I got to feel I was there vicariously as Shannon and Jackie tried to keep their little ones entertained during a very loooooong ceremony. Once Danny was stabilized, I was picked up by Jackie's mom-in-law, Laurinda, and went to Josh's graduation BBQ. Thank you, Jesus, for Josh only being an hour away from the hospital so I didn't have to miss all the graduation festivities. At the BBQ, I was able to give an update on Danny and was loved on by my kids and grandkids. Josh and Alisa shared the wonderful news of their first baby being on the way. I was grateful for the happy news. They asked us to pray because Alisa was having some issues. Little Ellie got a bloody nose and I thought, "I think I've seen enough blood to last a lifetime." Luke had painted me a Mother's Day picture and I got some flowers.

It was nice to see my children and grandchildren but now it was back to my current reality. Throughout the night, Danny had the dry heaves and bloody stools. I would rush to get him on the portable potty chair because I could get there faster than the nurses. I could not believe the intimate things I was having to do. This is what "In sickness and health" means. It's the hard stuff but you do it because you love each other.

Danny was so miserable over these next few days; I had never seen him so down--some of this was probably due to the meds he was on. I kept trying to say encouraging words to Danny and come at his beck and call. I was exhausted. This was our darkest hour.

The doctor put him on a heavier dose of anti-nausea medicine and pain killers. I came back from paying my daily $25 parking fee when Danny asked me if I had put the clothes in the dryer. "The clothes are wet." He said. I told him we haven't been home to do the laundry. I wondered if maybe he was feeling wet from sweating. He wasn't wet. Then he started talking about how everyone needed to work as a team. "They need to give an 'assist' when it is needed" (he wasn't watching sports). His Quinault blanket was coming apart so I told him I was going to sew it for him. As I walked away with the blanket, he got really upset and said, "Don't throw it to the seagulls!" I was worried about the crazy talk and went into the hall to tell the nurses. They reassured me that some delirium is normal. The meds plus the long stay in the hospital was causing it. The nurse came in and asked Danny some questions like, "What day is it?" I didn't even know the answer to that one because all the days were a blur. Danny answered the question correctly and I thought, "They probably think I'm the crazy one." I was slightly consoled that it was the meds affecting him, but had never heard my stable-minded husband talk this way. "How long can this last?" I wondered.

Sunday, May 8 From a CT scan, doctors determined there was a pseudo-aneurism on Danny's unblocked artery. They decided to do another angiogram procedure to unblock the aneurism. The surgeons ended up needing to fix three leaks and Danny was exposed to a lot of radiation. It seemed to do the trick because his bleeding lessened.

A light-hearted text conversation from my sis:

iMessage Message received from Cheryl Dean 5/9/2016 8:38:30 AM
They are having trouble doing blood draws. They have done it so much his veins are closing up. I think it's for self-preservation.

iMessage Message sent by Judy 5/9/2016 8:40:02 AM
I can hear their tiny voices now: "batten down the hatches, captain, pirates are coming to steal our goods!"

iMessage Message received from Cheryl Dean 5/9/2016 8:50:01 AM
Haha!!! I'm sure. The body does have interesting ways of protecting itself. They're saying, "you'll get no more blood out of me matey until you give some back". PS please pray that none of the blood they're giving him has HIV or AIDS

iMessage Message sent from Judy 5/9/2016 8:50:40 AM
I will! They are pretty careful about that nowadays!

And later Judy sent these encouraging words:

iMessage Message sent by Judy 5/10/2016 9:07:35 AM

"Blessed is the one who considers the poor! In the day of trouble the Lord delivers him; the Lord protects him and keeps him alive; he is called blessed in the land; you do not give him up to the will of his enemies. The Lord sustains him on his sickbed; and in his illness, you restore him to full health." Psalm 41:1-3 I have been praying for your husband very specific prayers asking for healing different parts of his body.

iMessage Message sent by Judy 5/10/2016 9:08:01 AM
Praying that God will sustain you! I love you, sis!

Tuesday, May 10 I was told the sad news that Alisa and Josh had lost their baby—7 weeks along. Lord, help them. I had had a dream a week or two before I found out they were expecting. I was in heaven in a grassy meadow when I saw a beautiful, brown-haired little girl who was so sweetly helping other children. I asked who that precious girl was. "It's Josh and Alisa's daughter," I was told. I believe that God was giving me a glimpse of the baby they will never get to hold until they meet her in heaven. I am happy to say that as I write this saga, a year after their loss, my son and daughter-in-law now have a bouncing baby boy. The Lord is the Great Redeemer.

When Danny was stable, we were moved to the 15th floor for the third time. Before we were moved out of acute care, a nurse prayed with me. By this time, Danny was receiving nutrition through his PIC line.

On the 15th floor we could see some of the same Virginia Mason nurses and PTs (patient technicians) we had had before: Becky, Kim, Ross, Kate and others who so lovingly took care of Danny's needs and even mine. Even though Danny's hospital bed and my cot were wedged together with little walking space, I didn't feel claustrophobic since I once again had a bird's-eye view of the Seattle skyline. Dr. Dennis came in and witnessed some of Danny's delirium as Danny gave a rambling speech on what made a good leader. He told me that he saw Rita dancing in the room. (Rita Bear Gray is a friend of ours who is a Native American dancer.) Danny was seeing her dancing in her white buckskin dress when he was actually looking at a picture of a sailboat on the hospital wall. Earlier Danny had talked about being adopted into the tribe. (We have been involved in ministry with Native Americans.) Since the doctor was there, I had a witness that I wasn't the delirious one. The doctor didn't seem too concerned though and verified it was probably the meds so he ordered a new prescription. He said some patients get so delirious, they think they are being held against their will. Now I knew why the patient in the room next to us would yell out, "Let me out of here!" a few times a day. Thankfully, the delirium subsided when the meds were changed. I was glad to have my Danny back…at least partially. His mind was there but his body had a long way to go.

The nurses and PTs continued to take good care of us. Since a criterion for going home was for Danny to be able to walk down the hall, we worked on this often. He health had improved greatly since he had been airlifted, but he was still so weak. While hooked up to the IV, Danny used a walker, the nurse pushed the IV stand, and I followed with a wheeled office chair—clickety, clack down the tiled hall. Danny would walk a few steps, then sit down in the chair. He'd walk a few more, then sit. At this pace, it was quite a feat to make it down the hall. The staff were becoming accustomed to seeing this tall guy with a gray pony tail in a hospital gown, taking baby steps down the hall. We cheered as Danny painstakingly added more steps between sits. One time, as we were taking our slow parade down the hall, we spotted our previous nurse, ThankGod. "ThankGod!" I called out. It sounded like I was praising God in the middle of the hall.

During this hospital stay, our "mate," Grant Russell, called long distance from Perth. He said I couldn't say "no" but he and his wife were setting up a Go Fund Me page with assistance from our friend Rachel Bertsch. He knew we were spending a lot of money on parking and I was already in the negatives with my school absences. Danny and I had been having a debate about me going back to Yakima so I could work since we were losing money. He had told me he would be fine, but I know he was just trying to be brave. I told him I needed to be by his side. Grant said to not worry about the missed days; they would be taken care of if the hospital is where God wanted me to be. I stayed with Danny, and with the generous gifts of family, friends, our church family, our needs were met. Money worries is an extra burden added to families with medical trauma. Thank you to all who helped lift this burden off our backs.

I spent some time in the 15th floor lounge as I continue to call in sick and send lesson plans to my school via email. It was a concern I wished I didn't have but it did give me something to occupy my mind. My regular life had to still go on even though my priority wasn't at the job. If Danny's hospital had been in Yakima and not three hours away, I would have been able to go into work while he was at the hospital. I drafted a letter with a time line of our visits to the hospital and my reasons for being away from school, along with a doctor's note verifying the hours in hopes that there would be a pool of donated hours in the school district. During my hospital strolls, I met a woman from Russia who now lived in Alaska. She had been at the hospital with her husband for a month. "Lord, how do people do this long term?" I wondered. "Father, give me enough strength to make it through each day as it comes."

Thursday, May 12 When I was returning from a dinner at a Chinese restaurant, I turned down a quaint Seattle street. Most of my travels were by foot because I didn't want to give up my parking spot by the Baroness Hotel—parking was a precious commodity and I didn't want to lose the time I had paid for. It was all a guessing game when I put money in the receptacle and I was unable to pay for more than a day at a time. I continued down the street admiring the red rhododendrons lining the old brick buildings. I wondered if I was listening to angels when I could faintly hear the sound of a choir. I followed the sound of the sweet, young voices until I traced the melody to beautiful stone church. I stood under the window where the choir was practicing and felt like the Lord had drawn me there to bless me and cheer my heart.

Friday, May 13 The Yakima School District approved me getting at least one sick day paid for from the company pool of absences. A dear teacher friend from Seattle Christian, Karen Stahlecker, came down from northern Washington for a visit along with her husband, Larry, and sweet mom, Grace. Karen and I had formed a special bond when we both taught at Seattle Christian and when I was there for her when she lost her first husband to cancer. They took me to IHOP for breakfast and encouragement. After hugs and goodbyes, these dear friends slipped me a card which I later found out had cash in it! That would cover some more of my missed work days. Praise God!

Around 9:30 that same evening, Danny had an excruciating attack of pain in his back! He kept saying, "Something is wrong. Something is wrong!!!" The nurse had changed the speed of his nutrition bag as per the doctor's orders.. I prayed over him and put my hand on his back. We wondered if Danny was going through a spiritual attack or if the speed of the meds was causing the pain. The nurse didn't think the speed of the meds could be a problem, but backed off the pace and the pain subsided. Before the pain had started, I had just texted all the contacts that Danny was doing great. I believe the prayers let up because they didn't feel there was a sense of urgency. I believe every prayer mattered.

Saturday, May 14 We continued to have visitors—so many people who loved us: Melvin and Becky Hoage, Jim and Beth Wulff, Bruce Cook, and John Anderson. While Bruce and John were in the room, the KCIA phone prayer meeting occurred. I loved listening to the conversation and even got to chime in with a little prophetic word. Bruce and John, like brothers to me, took me out for Thai food. Before they left, John had written on the white board where the medical information is updated. Under "discharge date," he wrote, "Today or Tomorrow." We got discharged the next day.

When we got back home, we tried to relax a bit. I still felt I should have a "bug-out bag" (as the military call it) so I could be ready to once again dash to Virginia Mason. Danny's friend, Dennis Crane, called and visited often bringing such a sweet spirit with him. The day we returned to Dad's House Church, Danny got a standing ovation. We were sure loved. On one of our church visits, Danny was able to walk weakly into the church, but after the service, he had to be wheeled out in a wheelchair which we borrowed from a friend who had already taken his mom to the car. Danny refused to use a walker at home and mostly sat on the couch watching the cooking channel to try to encourage his appetite. The channel made Naomi and me hungry so we were overeating.

For the next two months, it was a slow recovery process. Danny's re-sectioned digestive tract could take food now but Danny's mouth rebelled. As soon as Danny put food into his mouth, he would gag and sometimes even throw up. I tried all sorts of foods, tasteless food, baby food, smoothies, supplemental drinks—everything! I was disheartened that even his favorites which I usually cooked for him tasted bad to him. Even the smell of food made him sick. I tried to not take it personally that my cooking made him sick. Pastor Shawn, brought over another delicious meal. This time, Danny couldn't eat any of the food. On a good day, Danny could get down part of a ginger-ale and forced down a couple sips of Boost. Danny didn't even want to drink water. Our friend Stephanie continued to minister through foot massage and intercessory prayer. I saw Danny dwindle away before my very eyes. He looked like a starving person from a concentration camp—gaunt, boney; his cheeks were sunken in and his skin hung loose. After all he had been through to try to survive, I was afraid he was at the point where he could die of malnutrition!

Sunday, May 22 In the morning, I was trying to get down the stairs in the semi-darkness when I stumbled and fell. My shoulder ached and my toes felt sprained. This was the same foot I had broken twice. Now I had to hobble to help my patient.

George Muller once said, "The more I am in a position to be tried in faith with reference to my body, my family, my service for the Lord, my business, etc., the more shall I have opportunity of

seeing God's help and deliverance; and every fresh instance, in which He helps and delivers me, will tend towards the increase of my faith."
(Read more at: https://www.brainyquote.com/quotes/quotes/g/georgemull555664.html)

Monday, May 23 Naomi got baptized today at Dad's House. It was the first-year anniversary of Dad's House so the service was held outside. As Naomi stood in the dunking pool, the pastor asked Danny if he wanted to say any words. He didn't have the energy to stand so he sat nearby. His voice was very weak even though he was using a mic—but the speech was so sweet.

Thursday, June 2, I drove Danny over to Seattle for his checkup. Based on previous experiences, I decided to take a suitcase with me this time. Danny weighed in at 150 pounds—only 15 more pounds than me and he is 6' 2"! The doctors were horrified. They admitted Danny to the hospital and started him on a saline IV right away. Before the CAT scan, Danny had to drink this awful stuff even though he had difficulty swallowing anything. The scan showed everything in his abdomen to be normal. Meanwhile, he turned red and started itching terribly. He was given Benadryl since he appeared to be having an allergic reaction to the contrast drink.

Friday, June 3 Friday, Danny was to have a feeding tube put into his jejune (the part of the intestine normally connected to the duodenum which Danny no longer had). The surgeon planned on bypassing the stomach so food could pass the area of the surgery, thus avoiding nausea. I ventured down to the farmer's market in the street near the hospital while Danny had surgery. He was groggy when his bed was wheeled in by the technicians. Danny was so thin; the surgeon could shine a light from the endoscopy scope through Danny's stomach and he could see the light outside of his stomach so he would know where to make the insertion hole! Danny would still have to wait 24 hours before he could start receiving food through the tube hanging just below his belly button.

That evening, I met up with some teacher friends from my previous job as librarian at Seattle Christian School. We used to meet like this once a month so it was a joyful reunion and a break from the hospital. Danny texted me during the dinner saying that the docs had started him on food already. I texted back that he was going to be chubby by the time I got there. Before I left the restaurant, my friend, Jan Miller (who had already helped me through previous major life issues), slipped me a card with cash in it. I was so thankful that caring friends were generous so I didn't have to worry about money while facing my primary goal of keeping Danny alive and well.

Saturday, June 4 Danny woke up saying he felt better than he had for a long time. I slipped away to Laurinda's condo for breakfast, laundry, and a shower. While there, we facetimed my daughter Jackie and our shared grandchildren: Ellie and

Luke. I brought watermelon back to Danny but he could only get one bite down and didn't want to chance any more.

As before, the ability to walk the length of the hospital hall was one of the criterion for Danny getting released, so we practiced as often as he could. I pushed his IV pole, Danny walked with a walker, and the PCT, Marevic, walked behind Danny with an office chair with wheels so he could rest between steps—Danny, not the PCT. Sometimes it was literally just a few steps. Later in the evening, Danny walked to the waiting area with its fabulous view of Seattle which showed part of Lake Union and glimpse of Puget Sound. We just chatted and held hands. He had been so weak that our usual in-depth conversations had been rare. He said this was the best he had felt since before the first surgery.

I read the ingredients of Danny's tube-food and was shocked by the unhealthy ingredients--sugar, soy, canola oil--but knew the important thing at this point was to get some calories and vitamins into his frail frame. My patient/husband ate about eight bites of Raisin Bran (yahoo!), a bite of watermelon, and a bite of lemon meringue pie. The bran and watermelon weren't too bad but he said he couldn't take the lemon meringue pie…so I happily ate it. Stephanie Reiland sent us a text video with Pastor Shawn leading our church family in a rousing, "We love you Danny!" Then they yelled, "We love you Cheryl!" Then someone followed up with, "You're the best wife!" This made our day.

Sunday, June 5 Danny woke up at 2:00 am with horrible heart burn. He was still dealing with it when I woke up at 6:00. The pain was intense and to make things worse, he started having the dry heaves. He looked so miserable sitting in his hospital gown, holding on to a collapsible blue barf bag (EME bags). After scurrying around getting a doctor's prescription for GRD (gastro-reflux) meds and anti-nausea meds, the nurses finally gave him an anti-nausea shot so he could keep the pain pill for the GRD down. A few hours later, the chest/heartburn pain had subsided, but the incision from the feeding tube began to hurt. He was afraid he would throw up a pain pill so the nurses gave him a Dilaudid shot. Danny was going to need to stay at Virginia Mason until Monday so they could monitor his electrolytes.

Bruce Cook stopped in to our "penthouse" that afternoon. After some chatting, Bruce prophesied and prayed over Danny. The Lord gave him a vision of a Native American chief putting a full headdress on Danny. This was very encouraging for Danny. I left in the late afternoon so I could get home to be able to work Monday. My plan was to drive back to Seattle Monday night to bring my patient home.

Monday, June 6 Many of the students were awful that next day at school, challenging me as much as possible since it was the last week of school. I wanted to blurt out, "Don't you know what I've been through?!" but tried to keep myself calm. Even when a loved one is ill, the rest of life still goes on.

Deeper Still

As Emily said in the play, *Our Town*, "Do any human beings ever realize life while they live it? – every, every minute?" When a loved one is ill, it is now the most important focus in life; it's what matters. Allowing God to hold us in his grip and for us to hold tightly to Him is even more essential when life is in the balance or trauma enters our lives.

Carolyn and Ray Taylor graciously drove me to Seattle to pick Danny up. We stopped at a café in Cle Elum before Snoqualmie Pass and had a sweet conversation on the way. Danny was sitting on his hospital bed packed and anxious to leave his home away from home.

iMessage Message sent by Judy 6/8/2016 12:09:55 PM
I just encountered a description of you in my biblical counseling book. It used the word resilience. It is courageous endurance, heroism in the face of pain, the firm refusal to give up or give in, the brave determination to forge forward! That is you my beloved sis. I am so thrilled you are my sister!

iMessage Message received from Cheryl Dean 6/8/2016 3:22:18 PM
Oh thank you sweet sister! Pastor Toms told a story about a famous person—I think it was John Bunyan--who said the secret of his success was " I plod" I don't think I'm that skilled but I do plod. Not too coordinated; I just ripped open my arm while I was trying to move stuff around

in my classroom! I love you amazing, admirable sis

iMessage Message sent by Judy 6/8/2016 3:22:56 PM
Poor thing! May it heal quickly!

iMessage Message received from Cheryl Dean 6/8/2016 4:29:03 PM
Thanks Sis. Almost done here. I ran out of band aids so I hope I don't have any more injuries

I have been on steroids for 26 years so my skin is so thin, it bruises and tears easily. Praise God I didn't have any rheumatoid flares during these past four months. Jesus kept me upright even when I had sprained toes from the stair incident. I looked up the quote about plodding and discovered the author was the missionary, William Carey. When asked about the secret of his success, he said, "I can plod. I can persevere in any definite pursuit. To this I owe everything." (Read more at: https://www.brainyquote.com/quotes/quotes/w/williamcar404677.html)

Chapter 7

Staying Tethered – Cheryl

Sunday, June 19 I was writing in my journal in our prayer room on this day. It's a tiny room with French doors, a black leather counseling chair, a display case of family heirlooms and Native American memorabilia, and the red love seat upon which Danny gave me our first kiss. Counseling has gone on in this room along with deep meditation and prayer. Those who enter usually make a comment about how peaceful it feels in the room or how they can feel the Holy Spirit in the room. It is a room of solace, full of God's presence. Nearly every morning, Danny does his consecration prayer to God in this room. I made the following comments in my journal this particular morning as I sought direction in my life: "I took a big step in marrying Danny. That has affected the whole course of my life and any decisions I make from here on out. It is not just you and I, Lord, but we are now a three-some." At that point, I got a vision of Danny and me in a three-legged race—Jesus was the rope holding us together as we raced as a team. What one person does affects the other. Both trials and blessings will affect the other one. Then the Lord gave me a picture of a Venn diagram—He knew I would get this since I'm a language arts teacher. A Venn diagram is for comparing two things. Where the circles overlap is where the two things are alike. I realized as I drew the diagram, that the part where Danny and I overlap is God.

If I gathered up all the solid food Danny has eaten since his surgery on March 29, it would probably only fill one solitary plate! We had begun to take communion together nearly every evening. These times were a reminder of the sacrifice Jesus made for our salvation and our healing. We believed that having communion together was part of the healing process. At times, when Danny couldn't even get a morsel down, I would eat his unleavened cracker and drink his juice while I held his arm. That night, he took a miniscule piece of cracker, I could barely see it in his fingers, as he dipped it slightly into the juice. That was all he could handle. The oncologist's nutritionist believed his eating problem stemmed from his thick saliva so she recommended a glycerin mouth rinse and eating spicy foods. This advice helped only slightly.

After all that Danny had survived, was food going to be the thing that does him in? Is he just afraid to eat? I tried to not dwell on those anxious thoughts and instead laid my husband on the altar before the Lord and, as Danny's helpmate, wrote this prayer for his healing in my journal: "Lord, help him! He has been through a nine-hour surgery, an abdominal infection, internal bleeding twice, throwing up massive amounts of blood, a life flight and two ambulance rides to Seattle, and six admissions to the hospital for 3-10 days at a time. You have brought him through all of that, Lord, and yet, he has not been able to eat. How can a person survive without eating? Is he destined to be fed a tan, milky substance through his intestine the rest of his days? Is he destined to be tethered to the tube and the stand which holds up the bag? Will he ever gain his weight back? Will he ever gain his strength back? Will he ever be able to take a walk with me or ever be able to be intimate with me? Will he be able to speak again? Will he be able to travel?

"Lord, you said he would get through this. I am so thankful he made it through a very difficult surgery and many traumatic events. Now I am asking that you continue to get him through by helping him eat. If you can cause a blind man to see; if you can help a cripple man to walk; if you can cause a dead man to rise; then surely you can heal whatever is preventing Danny from eating. Lord, please! I call upon that same power that raised Jesus from the grave to flow over Danny and give him the ability to eat and nourish himself.

"So many people have offered up prayers for Danny. Surely You have heard everyone. Surely You love Danny and want him healed. Maybe we just have to walk it out a little more. Lord Jesus, we want to wait on You, Your perfect will, Your perfect timing; but we are desperate for Your will. Please act on my husband's behalf!"

Monday, June 20 More from my journal: "Please heal my husband. Heal him outright or give us wisdom. I cannot do anything in my own strength. We are relying wholly on You Jesus. I'm going to keep reading the Word until You speak to me either through your Word or Your Spirit." I then began to look through *The Living Bible* given to me by my Grandmother and Granddaddy Owens at my high school graduation in 1974. Things that I had underlined in my early college and career life were now ringing true to me this day and were filling me with faith that we have a good God who does no wrong.

"See, God has come to save me! I will trust and not be afraid for the Lord is my strength and song; He is my salvation." (Isaiah 12: 2-3)

"He will give you the strength to endure." (2 Corinthians 1:7)

"We felt we were doomed to die and saw how powerless we were to help ourselves; but that was good, for then we put everything into the hands of God, who alone could save us, for He can even raise the dead." (2 Corinthians 1:9)

"And because the king trusts in the Lord, he will never stumble, never fall; for he depends upon the steadfast love of God who is above all gods." (Psalm 21:7)

I prayed, "Lord, show us you love us! We depend on your steadfast love."

I love how the Psalmist tells it like it is. First, they tell about their plight: "I'm in the pit of despair." Then tell about their rescue: "Praise you for saving me!" Psalm 22: 14-15, 19, 24-26 especially struck me as appropriate for what we were going through. "My strength has drained away like water, and all my bones are out of joint. My heart melts like wax;

my strength has dried up like sunbaked clay; **my tongue sticks to my mouth,** for you have laid me in the dust of death…O Lord, don't stay away. O God my Strength, hurry to my aid. Rescue me from death…Let all Israel sing his praises, for he has not despised my cries of deep despair; he has not turned and walked away. When I cried to him, he heard and came. **Yes, I will stand and praise you before all the people. I will publicly fulfill my vows in the presence of all who reverence your name.** The poor **shall eat and be satisfied:** all who seek the Lord shall find him and shall praise his name. Their hearts shall rejoice with everlasting joy. The whole earth shall see it and return to the Lord; the people of every nation shall worship him."

A thought hit me that I should paraphrase this Psalm with Danny in it, so I prayed this prayer: "Why does it seem like You have forsaken my husband? Lord, come to Danny's aid. His bones are out of joint. His tongue sticks to the roof of his mouth. His saliva is thick and he cannot get nourishment past that formidable, dry gateway. His strength has waned. Fat has disappeared from his body, and his muscles have atrophied as nutrients have been leeched from them. Danny's strength has dissipated like a dry well. He can barely walk through his own home. Without nourishment, he will be laid in the dust of death's door. You have been his strength for all these years. Rescue him from death and spare his precious life. You, O Lord, are good. We will continue to sing your praises because we fear and reverence your name. Even though we are still in the thick of the battle for

Danny's life, you have not turned and walked away. We are crying to you. You hear us and come when we need you. Even though it doesn't feel like you are here; you are still here. You are still in this situation and are already acting behind the scenes. Lord, you have proven yourself faithful before and we can trust you now. Your Spirit told us that Danny would get through this; we stand on your faithfulness."

"Soon the day will come when we will stand and praise you before the people. In the presence of other believers, Danny and I will publicly tell of your goodness and how you saved him. The day will come when Danny will eat and be satisfied. Your word, O Lord, has said that all who seek the Lord shall find him and shall praise his name. That is what we will do, Father. Our hearts shall rejoice with everlasting joy. In fact, the whole world will hear of our testimony and will return to the Lord. Our friends in Australia, Canada, United Kingdom, Las Vegas, Iowa, Chicago, Texas, California, Idaho, Seattle, and Yakima will see your goodness Lord and will worship you!" [As I write this, Danny is on a tour of Israel where I am sure his is proclaiming the goodness of the Lord.]

It was so uplifting to pray the Psalm with Danny in it, I decided to paraphrase Psalm 23: "Because the Lord is Danny's shepherd, he has everything he needs to sustain life. Danny rests on the couch and regains his strength as he looks outside at the flowers and birds which God has also sustained. God restores Danny's failing health. Even in

Danny's weakness, God helps him do what honors him most. Even during those times when Danny was near death and life-flighted to the hospital, he was not afraid because Jesus was there with him. God's comfort has followed him through every hospital stay, every procedure, and every ambulance ride. The Lord has provided Danny with the food of His world even when his own body rejected the food of this world. The Lord's blessings have overflowed to Danny and me: loving notes and visits from friends, financial gifts to help the loss of income, healing foot rubs, the lawn mowed, shower head repaired, the blessings spoken over him, and the comfort of a soft Quinault blanket. God's goodness and unfailing kindness will stay with Danny all his life. And when Danny is old and his life is over, he will live with his Savior forever in his heavenly home."

I then sat next to Danny and prayed the prayer over him. I would encourage readers to find a meaningful passage and paraphrase it to fit you or your sick loved one.

Sunday, June 26 It was now 20 days since Danny had his feeding tube inserted. He still had only gained five pounds, but at least he wasn't losing weight. Danny was still hardly eating anything by mouth. Food bags were hung on a pole (a weaker version of the hospital models) and slowly dripped into his tube. He not so fondly called his feeding tube, his "tether." Because Danny was achy and nauseous, the nutritionist recommended that I put a syringe of water into his tube. Naomi and I tagged team with this. Stephanie continued to use her healing hands to massage Danny's feet with essential oils. As she massaged, she prayed for Danny's healing. I believe this was an instrumental part of his healing process.

Wednesday, June 29 Danny went to the capitol of Washington in Olympia which was his first big outing since March. He, Dennis and Paul were at a rally where Franklin Graham, Billy Graham's son, spoke. Franklin was going from capitol to capitol in each state praying for all to be unified in prayer for our country especially with the upcoming election. Danny brought a folding chair because he was still so weak and left his "tether" at home. The doctors said he wasn't getting enough nutrients if he used the feeding tube for only part of the day so he encouraged Danny to use it at least 16 hours! Danny figured he could go a few hours without the tube so he could go to Olympia.

On this particular day, I was again using *The Living Bible* for my quiet time, and divinely found this verse: "Live in vital union with him. Let your roots grow down into him and draw up nourishment from him. See that you go on growing in the Lord, and become strong and vigorous in the truth you were taught. Let your life overflow with joy and thanksgiving for all he has done." (Col. 2:6)

As I meditated on this verse, the words 'vital union' really hit me. We are to have vital union, not just a weak connection, a quick thought that says, "O yah, God is near me...somewhere." But we are to have a 'vital union.' I was wondering what vital really meant so, as every great scholar does, I checked out Webster's Dictionary. Vital union is defined as: "extremely important, needed by your body in order to keep living. Of the utmost importance." I discussed with the Lord how intimacy, a vital relationship with him, was of utmost importance but I didn't always have it, or make time for it. But we need this vital union to be able to live and move and have our being. In the movie, *Gravity*, Sandra Bullock is an engineer on a spaceship. While she is making repairs on the outside of the spaceship, her tether breaks. She screams into her helmet microphone, "I'm detached! I'm detached!" Then she is spun through space until she finally stops—far away from her spaceship. She now floats through outer space with no aim, no direction. She doesn't even know which way she is facing. I can hardly think of anything more horrifying.

Why are we not horrified when we become detached from God? I continued to write in my journal, "Lord Jesus, without our connection to You, we are floating without direction. Lord, I want to be intimate with You. I want to have vital, life sustaining union with You!" These thoughts got me thinking about Danny being tethered to his food source 16 hours a day. Since he rarely ate anything by mouth (and hadn't for three months), he would die without the feeding tube. Danny was in vital union with the feeding tube. Likewise, Danny stays connected to the Holy Spirit in daily reading of the Word, praying, consecrating himself, and seeking the will of God. He is rooted and grounded in the

Lord and is becoming strong and vigorous in the truth he is learning. For Danny is joined together by Christ's strong sinews and he grows only as he gets his nourishment and strength from God. (Colossians 2:19, Living)

Friday, July 8 Danny was still hardly eating anything by mouth and was still attached to the feeding tube contraption. As he went through this grueling season, I prayed that when Danny could not eat regular food, he would be able to feast on the Word of the Lord. As Danny's wife who intimately knows him and witnesses his character on the home front where people tend to let their hair down and their true character out, I knew Danny had the same character at home and was obedient to God's every word. He read the Bible every day and diligently listened to God's voice. Why wasn't this eating aversion healed?

In home group the evening before, Danny seemed more himself and taught a great lesson about spiritual warfare. He had a stronger voice even though he was still extremely skinny and underweight. The feeding tube was keeping Danny alive, but not helping him put on any meat. He still had to wear sweatpants or pajama bottoms which his bony frame barely held up. (One night, in a show of comradery, I asked our home group friends to show up in pajama bottoms.) Danny's face was gaunt and sunken in, but his long dimples were still there. His thighs were only as thick as his bones. He was as skinny as Ichabod Crane.

It had been prophesied over Danny that he still had so much work up ahead to do for the Lord. He had had a vision of Heaven where he was handed a box which held all of his future assignments. I pleaded with the Lord, as His daughter, that He would heal my husband. I prayed that my Father would give him the ability to eat and to regain muscle and strength. I prayed that my Father would prepare Danny for the work He still had for him to do on this earth.

"But your heavenly Father already knows perfectly well that you need them, and he will give them to you if you give him first place in your life and live as he wants you to." (Matthew 56:23, Living)

I was feeling touchy and grumpy around this time which I thought was strange because all the hospital runs and near-death experiences seemed behind us and my husband was still alive. Along with the trauma being behind us, the extreme stress I was experiencing the past school year was over for the summer. Danny was now in maintenance mode. I was kept busy with making Danny's food bags and meds, making the extended family dinner (Naomi's son was now living with us), taking classes to keep my teaching certificate, but I was not under the adrenaline stress I had recently experienced. Shouldn't I be breathing a sigh of relief, enjoying life because my husband was alive?

As a wife and caregiver, my mind, body, and emotions had been spent. My adrenaline had been pumping out when I needed it and now I felt exhausted. I hadn't had time to properly process everything while I went through it so I was processing it now. I kept trying to find a reason for my depression: new family members living with us, a broken dish, missing the recycling…It was a vicious cycle of trying to blame crazy little things for my sadness when I logically knew I should be happy. Friends told me these feelings were normal after trauma, and I finally realized that what I was experiencing was Post Traumatic Stress Disorder. I thought PTSD was more something people who had been in war or who had been abused would experience. Now I realize any kind of trauma can cause some level of PTSD, even to a caregiver.

This was one of my prayers: "Jesus, help me through this. Miraculously heal me of the horrible memories of the events I have been through. Thank you for getting me through them with strength, level-headedness, and clarity. Now I pray there are no more ill effects. Help me to not take it out on my family. Let my adrenal gland heal along with my stress belly! Most importantly, let my heart heal."

At that moment, a firetruck came into our court. My heart jolted with the memories of two other visits, but I reassured myself that it wasn't there for my husband this time. I realized that healing from PTSD wasn't going to happen overnight. "Lord help me stay in the secret place. Even though Post Traumatic Stress is a common occurrence, don't let it be common for me. Heal me supernaturally."

Chapter 8

Miracle Healing – Danny

On July 8th, I felt impressed to go to a local worship meeting being led by our dear friend, Dr. Sunny Bhaskaran. We came into the sanctuary and I sat in the second seat in for some reason even though I almost always sit on the aisle. Although it was a typical hot Yakima summer night, I felt very weak and very cold.

The worship began and Cheryl could not see the words for the worship songs and she decided to stand elsewhere so she could see the words and enter into the worship. As I sat there with eyes closed and my hands in worship, Dr. Sunny came and sat in the empty chair. He took my hand and began to pray over me. Suddenly he declared with authority, "You spirit of Anorexia come off of him." I couldn't believe my ears. "What did he say? Anorexia?" There is no way I could have had any idea of the spirit that was behind my inability to eat. The fact is, something did lift off me and I immediately wanted to go to Dairy Queen for a chocolate sundae!

When Cheryl came back to her seat, I told her, "You are not going to believe what just happened!" I excitedly shared the words Dr. Sunny had prayed over me and how the spirit of anorexia had lifted. Something had broken. I realized that I had become afraid to eat and I had no desire to eat at all. I also realized there was a change and I wanted to eat.

The next day I told Cheryl, "Let's find a Thai Restaurant." I had a taste for Tom Yum Soup.

Sunday, July 10th This was my first true meal in the three and half months and the first time Cheryl and I had been out to eat since the beginning of this ordeal. I looked a bit different than I did in early March. Having lost 63 pounds and now having a 31-inch waste, I couldn't even wear my wedding ring because it would slip off my finger.

We had turned the corner and now there was real hope that I would get well and regain my strength. Over the next few weeks my body slowly began to adjust to eating solid food. At first, only a few bites would be enough to make me feel full.

With the feeding tube in place and the addition of solid food, I slowly added a few more pounds and gained more strength.

Over the next few weeks and as more weight was coming back, my hope began to rise for the day when the feeding tube would be removed from my abdomen.

Finally, on August 3rd, we began our trip to Seattle. The goal was to be there by 11:30. Unknown to us there was a major accident on the freeway from Yakima to Seattle. As a result, we arrived at the hospital in Seattle at 3:15. The two and half hour drive became six-and-a-half hours, an all-day ordeal.

Dr. Alseidi, the same surgeon who had performed the surgery 128 days previously, was surprised at how well I looked. When he asked what had changed, we explained that through prayers, a miracle had happened. The doctor shook his head and said, "Well, I can't compete with that!" He was happy to be removing the feeding tube. Then, like a man pulling weeds, the doctor took a hold of the tube and said, "Now bear with me." Ouch Ouch!!!! and out came the tube. The doctor literally just pulled it out. Cheryl and I joke around now about my second belly button.

Daily I gained my strength and continued to add more and more solid food items to my diet. As the months passed, I added even more items to my diet with the exception of pizza and hamburgers. But if it was spicy, it was great. I'm so loving Mexican food.

Cheryl—Our bedroom window faces rolling sagebrush hills. After this past 4th of July, teens playing with fireworks, caught the hill on fire and a big swath of land was burned to a crisp. Throughout the months, we viewed a huge black square on the yellow hill except for when it was covered by snow—which happened quite often this particular winter. After the snow melted, this once charred piece of land proved to be greener than the rest of the hill. I knew that ash added nutrients to the soil but I learned later that fire also purified soil. This is what God has done with our challenges this past year. Our sorrows, and strains, and darkest nights, have renewed us to new life. We are better than we would have been without the fire.

Danny--Today, Cheryl and I are looking forward to all that God has planned for the next chapters in our lives. We know that we are here for a reason and our goal is to embrace all of life and fulfill our destiny.

We are determined to never waste our sorrows and always look for Jesus in every situation.

Chapter 9

The End of the Valley

It would be wonderful if everything ended on a high note; however, life goes on. After many months of physical and emotional pain greater than anyone could imagine, there was a battle yet to be won.

I had spent so many months of being like a wet towel that has been twisted into a knot and pulled until every drop of water has been wrung out. I had spent so many months on Opiate pain killers and a variety of medications to help me survive. After everything was said and done, the pain left me affected in the deepest places of my emotions and soul.

As an example, after a funeral, the hardest time is not at the funeral or even a few days after, but it is weeks or months later when everyone has gone home and you are all alone with your thoughts and the feelings that are yours and yours alone.

After all the physical pain and all the emotional pain of the last few months and after all the prayer covering had lifted due to the healing that was now manifesting, I found myself wanting one more glass of wine than normal. It was the agony of the private pain of the soul that remained somewhat hidden but very much there.

Now a new battle had to be faced. Now it was just me and the remnant of sorrow and grief that was there for so many months. Now it was facing life again without pain medication or that extra glass of wine, and the realization that my body was affected by all the medications originally used to ease the suffering.

Now it was time to face life on its own terms. Now it was living on the realities of my faith again and trust in the Grace of God that got me through the trauma. Now it was walking in the knowledge of His constant care without adding any other physical support for the body and soul that suffered so much.

Now the love of God and His constant friendship become the air I breathe. I am like a man two hundred feet under water; He is my oxygen tank and the only way I stay alive.

Jesus was the reality during the greatest pain, obstacles, complications, and agony of soul. Jesus was the answer then and is the answer now during this time of adjustment to a life of health and freedom from all medications.

Tomorrow go down against them. Behold, they will come up by the ascent of Ziz, and <u>you will find them at the end of the valley</u> in front of the wilderness of Jeruel. (II Chronicles 20:16, NASB)

After all the warfare, struggles and the intensity of the crisis, there is just life. Oftentimes it is at the end of the ordeal that some of the greatest personal battles must be fought. It is at this time, alone, when you find out who you really are and the fruit if there is any, depending on whether you grew from your sorrows or whether you wasted them. When you are all alone at 2:00 a.m. and you wake up with the memories and feelings of so many months of trauma then Jesus becomes more than a thought. He is your counselor, friend, companion and the God I love and cherish.

After so many months had passed, I found my emotions rising and had a deep sense of uneasiness. This emotional state was so out of character. What became clear one morning at 3:30 a.m. was that I was suffering with PTSD (Post-Traumatic Stress Disorder). Once this came to the surface, I could face the emotional trauma that resulted from the events described in this book. Slowly over the months of talking openly about my feelings and processing the emotions, this too lifted. During this time, I took time out from the Italian part of me that enjoys a glass of wine and from anything else that would distract me from the task at hand-the healing of my heart and mind. It was a time to reflect and allow all the emotions to rise to the surface. Face them and walk through them.

I shared with my friends and family what I was going through and included them in the process of healing emotionally.

It also became clear that one trigger for PTSD was going to the Oncologist for my quarterly testing to make sure the cancer had not returned. There was never a time when I felt alone or felt fear; however, simply walking through a process like this takes its toll in the deep places of the heart and emotions.

Through it all, my wife never relented in her care, love, and confidence that I would be ok.

I have grown in so many ways and now my hope is that after you have heard our story you will choose life in every situation and never waste your sorrows.

I have learned that freedom begins when we stop playing tug of war with God over the pains, disappointments, and frustrations of life. When we stop trying to cajole God into performing up to our expectations. When we reach the end of our rope and hit the wall of the worst-case scenario and break through to the other side, this is where true freedom begins. When we step though the veil of adversity, hopelessness, and our greatest fears do we find real life, free of all doubts, fears and unbelief. We are now living the unencumbered life of total trust in God. We now know the fact that He is a good God and will always be regardless of our circumstances. We now know more than ever that everything works out for good for those who love God and are called according to His purposes.

There truly is no pit so deep that His love isn't deeper still.

Weeping may last for the night, but a shout of **joy *comes* in the morning.**

Psalm 30:5b (NASB)

Life Goes on! –

I have regained half my weight loss.

Our passion for life rises higher every day!

Thank you all for praying!

And thank you for listening to our story.

Sioux Prayer

**Native American Prayer said
when you have finished all your words**

Mitakuye Oyasin

"All my Relations"

Epilogue

Almost a year after our trial began, Cheryl and I went out for dinner on Valentine's day 2017 and discovered our friend, Angela Sprester, who is a seer prophet, at the restaurant. We had a great time of sharing and catching up and then she revealed something that stunned us both. Angela visited our home in mid-March of 2016 to join in the meeting we were holding in our home with Lana Vawser.

Now, we had shared with only a very few people the fact that I would be going in for surgery and that we had found out I had cancer only days before.

Angela had abruptly left the meeting that day and we had wondered what had happened to cause her to leave so quickly.

This is why:

She shared that during the meeting she had seen a vision of herself and Cheryl standing at my casket. She immediately left the meeting and began calling numerous prayer warriors and asked them to have emergency prayer for me. She told them, without knowing anything about my medical condition, "If we don't pray, Danny is going to die."

This early alert sent many people to their knees in intercession for me. We had no idea that this had happened until our divine meeting with Angela. It was clear the Lord sent out the early warning signal on my behalf.

When we shared Angela's vision with our home group, friends immediately jumped up and began to declare that no remnant of the vision would be allowed to exist in any form. We prayerfully closed the circle on this event in my life.

As Dr. Bruce Cook stated, my survival and ultimately my healing was a team effort.

We are so grateful for the fact that hundreds of people around the world went to prayer.

Now we know why so many people we have never met sent us their commitment to pray. The need was that urgent. The network extended far beyond our immediate friends and family as person after person passed the prayer request to their circle of friends, church groups, and fellowships.

We are humbled by this outpouring of love and the Grace of our King, Lord and Friend, Yeshua, Jesus Christ.

Made in the USA
Columbia, SC
12 January 2018